IN REMEMBRANCE OF ME

IN REMEMBRANCE OF ME

by

DAVID CAIRNS

1967

GEOFFREY BLES · LONDON

© DAVID CAIRNS, 1967

Printed in Great Britain
by Cox & Wyman Ltd., Fakenham, Norfolk
Published by
GEOFFREY BLES, LTD
52 DOUGHTY STREET, LONDON W.C.1.
33 YORK STREET, SYDNEY
531 LITTLE COLLINS STREET, MELBOURNE
70–2 EAGLE STREET, BRISBANE
C. M. L. BUILDING, KING WILLIAM STREET, ADELAIDE
LAKE ROAD, NORTHCOTE, AUCKLAND
100 LESMILL ROAD, DON MILLS, ONTARIO
POST BOX 420, BARBADOS
P.O. BOX 8879, JOHANNESBURG
P.O. BOX 834, CAPE TOWN
P.O. BOX 2800, SALISBURY, RHODESIA

To

the Minister and Kirk Session of
St. Giles Cathedral, Edinburgh

CONTENTS

Introduction

Some time ago the Minister and Kirk Session of St. Giles Cathedral in Edinburgh invited me to give a series of addresses there on the Sacrament in Holy Week. In his invitation, Dr. Whitley asked me "to try to do for the twentieth century what Robert Bruce had done for the men of his time in the sixteenth".

This Robert Bruce was minister of the High Kirk of St. Giles in the days of King James the Sixth and First, and on five Sundays of February and March 1589 he preached five sermons in the Cathedral which have become famous in Scotland and beyond, as expressing the finest type of Post-Reformation sacramental doctrine of the Scottish Church.

It was with some sense of awe and privilege that I agreed to the invitation, with a thought also of all those who in the centuries between had taken part in worship at the Sacrament in this building. A study of Bruce's sermons made me realise afresh how much the whole situation had changed since his day. At that time, barely thirty years after the Scottish Reformation, there were still many living who had grown up in the pre-Reformation Church, and there was in the sermons, naturally and necessarily, a certain polemical note and a sharp criticism of Roman Catholic doctrine and practice.

But we are today living in an unbelievably different

theological climate, and there seemed to be many other good reasons why such a series of sermons might be timely now, and why in modified form the material contained in them might be published with advantage. For since the sixteenth century an enormous amount of linguistic and historical work has been done on the New Testament and its background, so that we have now immense new resources for a better understanding of the origins and character of the Sacrament. Further, there has been a great wealth of study on sacramental doctrine, whose aim has been a better understanding of the different viewpoints of the Churches, and it can be claimed that a considerable *rapprochement* has taken place between various standpoints which at the time of the Reformation were uncompromisingly opposed to one another.

Yet this work has for the greater part remained buried in scholarly and often abstruse volumes, and the insight and inspiration to be drawn from it has too little been made available to the general public. My aim in giving the sermons, and in putting together the book which results from them, has been to make available for intelligent non-specialist readers some of the wonderful insights which scholars have recently given us, or recovered for us. In the matter of style, in preparing the matter for book form I have tried to retain something of the directness of approach natural to a spoken address, while removing forms of speech that are suited only to a situation where a speaker sees his audience sitting before him. I ask the reader's indulgence if he feels that I have not quite succeeded in securing the right balance.

The public whom I have had in mind all through, are people who like myself wish better to understand and appropriate the great gift offered to us in sacramental worship, people who want to take part in it worthily, and who are often worried as to what they can today believe and accept.

I have further had in mind the hope that what I have set down might be of help to ministers who wish to preach about the Sacrament, and who have also to instruct young communicants about it. I have long been struck by the inadequacy of manuals on this subject, and I know that many others share my opinion here.

My aim has accordingly been to speak rather to the heart than the analytical intellect, and to avoid terms remote from common experience as far as possible. I have tried not to shirk real issues, but I have also tried, on the whole, to affirm rather than to deny, to lay weight on those things that unite Churches of differing traditions, and to express in simple language the general beliefs of that part of the Christian family to which most of my hearers and I belonged, the Presbyterian Church.

I have endeavoured to acknowledge, as far as suits such a book, the authorities from whom I have quoted, but I must particularly mention my indebtedness to two contemporary writers, Joachim Jeremias and Gustav Aulen, whose books *The Eucharistic Word of Jesus* and *Eucharist and Sacrifice*, have been a stimulus and an inspiration to me. It may be thought that I am too dependent on these two writers, but I would assure the reader that my reading has covered a considerable field, and that I have chosen from that field what I found most helpful.

The subject is extraordinarily close-knit, and it has been hard to deal with each of the five themes considered in the five chapters, without at once going on to another. The chapters deal with five aspects of the Lord's Supper. The first considers its origins in the Old Testament Passover Feast, and the light thrown upon the Sacrament by the character of the Passover, which looked back with gratitude to a mighty historical deliverance. The second chapter tries to indicate the nature of the presence of Christ in the Supper, and the gift received in it by the believer and the Church. The third treats not only of the fellowship in the Supper between Christ and the individual, but between Christ and the Church, between the members of the Church, and between the Church and the blessed dead. The fourth sets forth a view of the Sacrament in which Christ's sacrifice is present, not as an offering of the Church to God, but as God's gift to it, perfect and complete, on the strength of which the Church dares to share in the intercession of the Son. And the fifth chapter emphasises the forward look of the Sacrament to the day when "the human race will be home, gathered round the Father's table, after Iliads and Odysseys yet to be".

CHAPTER I

The Lord's Supper as a Memorial

If a visitor wholly ignorant of Christian traditions were to come today from outer space, or indeed from a wholly secular land, and to enter one of our churches, and to see there the central act of Christian worship, how very strange it would appear to him! Whether he saw it in its most ornate form in the Roman or Orthodox Mass, with choral music and incense, or in the austere form which can still be seen today in the remoter Scottish highlands, he would probably conjecture that this was something which had its roots very deep in the past. If he did, he would be right, for this custom and rite has lasted for nearly two thousand years. And if we trace its origins indirectly back to the Jewish Passover, we can date its ancestry as being some fifteen hundred years older still.

It is with this central act of Christian worship and its meaning that I propose to deal in the pages that follow. We know that the Communion Service has its origin in actions done by Jesus on the night of his betrayal when he took supper with his disciples in the upper room in Jerusalem. Here we are standing on very firm ground historically. There are many stories told about Jesus in the Gospels whose authenticity the sceptic can question. But the fact that he broke the bread and poured out the wine is, I suppose, about as well authenticated as the fact of his historical existence – a question on which no serious scholar of today is in doubt.

This central act of our Christian worship has received different names in the different Churches of Christendom – Roman Catholics and the Orthodox Church call it the Mass, the typical Anglican name is perhaps the Holy Communion or Eucharist, while Presbyterianism has called it by preference the Lord's Supper. And for all the important differences in the shape of the rite and its interpretation, there is a great central unity which has at times almost been lost sight of in the heat of controversy.

Yet we must admit that since the Lord's Supper has been from the first a focus of attention, there has been almost endless discussion on nearly every point with which this book will deal, and even with regard to the nature of the meal at which Jesus sat down with his disciples on the night of his betrayal. What was its nature? Was it a Passover Feast, or was it a meal like those shared together by the members of Jewish religious fellowships at much more frequent intervals than the yearly Passover Feast? Such customs were not infrequent at the time of Christ. For some years it was generally agreed among scholars that it was such a fellowship meal, and not the Passover. Into the pros and cons of this elaborate discussion I luckily do not need here to enter. All that I need to say is that today there is a growing agreement that it was actually the Passover Feast of which Jesus and his disciples partook. Therefore something about that Feast must be said here, for this will help us much to understand what Jesus did and meant when he broke the bread, and gave it, and the wine, to his disciples.

The Passover was a yearly festival at which the families of Israel commemorated their great deliverance in days long past from their captivity in Egypt. The story of this deliverance, however embroidered with legendary detail, was the historical basis of Israel's existence as a nation in covenant with God. The feast, which fell at the time of the Passover full moon in the spring, was an occasion of solemn remembrance, thanksgiving and joy. Though celebrated by families in their homes and not in the Temple, it was also a national feast. All those who were able, came to Jerusalem, and the city was full of visitors. A solemn ritual was observed at the feast, and it probably varied but little. One man in each household acted as the President, most commonly the father of the family. It was usual for men, women and children to share in it, but it was also possible for a group of men, like Jesus and his disciples, to sit down together.

The main dish was the Passover Lamb. The book of *Exodus* (Chapter 12) tells us that the people had been instructed by God to kill a lamb for each family, and to sprinkle its blood upon their doorposts. It is probable that this rite and this feast came out of the still more distant past, but what happened in Egypt on the eve of the Exodus was this. This rite of sprinkling and this feast were given a new historic significance, as commemorating God's mighty liberation of his people from captivity in Egypt. And Israel never forget the terror and the wonder of that night, the deliverance rushing through the darkness, the sudden journey, the enemy pursuing and overthrown, the Egyptians lying dead upon the seashore.

What was the ritual of the Passover Feast? Before the meal began, special prayers were said.[1] On the table, as well as the lamb, there was unleavened bread, a dish of bitter herbs, and a fruit *puree*, of the colour and consistency of clay. To each of these dishes in the feast a special significance was attached. And at one point the youngest member of the family was instructed to make formal inquiry of the meaning of all the observances of that night – and answers were given by the father of the family. He rehearsed again the meaning of the whole feast, and its solemn and joyful origin in God's tremendous deliverance in the distant past. The reply was given that the Passover Lamb is eaten "because God passed over the houses of our fathers in Egypt". Unleavened bread is eaten because "This is the bread of misery which our fathers ate in Egypt", while the bitter herbs were compared with the slavery endured in Egypt, and so on. And the guests reclined at table, as a symbol that they had been given the joy and dignity of freedom by this great deliverance.

But for the men of the Old Testament, the Passover Feast was something more than a remembering, however valid, of what God had done in the past. It was not without the providence of God that the Feast was given this solemn interpretation, and there can be no doubt that behind the unleavened bread, the bitter herbs, and the

[1] For much of the material in this chapter, see *Jeremias, Eucharistic Words of Jesus*. First Edition. (Oxford 1955). E.T., esp. pp. 58–60.

Passover lamb, each guest, as it has been said, "could discern a reality which his eyes could not see, and which his mouth did not eat".

For the Passover was a Covenant Feast, and to eat at table at such a feast was one of the most solemn ways of entering into a covenant, or renewing it. God was present, and by eating together thus in his presence and at his command, the guests entered afresh into the Covenant with him, just as truly as did those who ate together in Egypt on the dark night of deliverance. By this act of his and theirs, God united them with himself as members of his people, and united them with one another in that fellowship. The Passover was for each successive generation a feast of communion between God and his people *now*.

This ritual feast, was thus not merely a looking back to the historic deliverance of Israel in the past, but neither was its significance exhausted when to that memory there was added the awareness of encounter with God in the present. As time went on, its participants more and more looked forward to the great event of the future, the coming of the longed-for Messiah.

> O come, O come, Immanuel,
> And ransom captive Israel!

There was an old tradition that the Messiah would come on the night of the Passover. And, since there was a tradition that Elijah would come again as the forerunner of the Messiah, there grew up later the practice of leaving a vacant place at the table for Elijah.

Thus, for the Jews, the Passover Feast spanned the

whole mighty arch of history in grateful memory and urgent hope. Even today these words of Exodus are vibrant after so many thousand years: "And this day shall be unto you for a memorial, and ye shall keep it as a feast by an ordinance for ever, . . . it is a night much to be observed unto the Lord." We shall see later how this threefold pattern, strung upon the loom of the past, the present, and the future, has been carried over to the Lord's Supper.

Now when Jesus sat down with the disciples in the upper room to eat the Passover, this whole ritual observance and its dear and sacred significance was familiar to them, and the New Testament accounts do not describe the details of what they did, so far as they followed the customs of the Passover Feast, for these details were familiar to the people who first read the Gospels, as they are not familiar to Gentile readers today.

But certain things are mentioned in the narratives, a certain strange and unexpected turn to Christ's actions which startled the disciples, and certain mysterious words with which he interpreted these actions. And yet these acts, and these interpretative words, would be illumined for the disciples by their knowledge of the Passover Ritual which I have explained. What Jesus said and did now was indeed new and strange, but they were accustomed to this *kind* of action and interpretation from their familiarity with the Passover ritual.

After the first dishes, the *hors d'oeuvres* of bitter herbs and the fruit *puree*, there came a grace before the main course, which was the Passover Lamb. It was at this point that Jesus made the first unexpected innovation in the

Passover Ritual which is recorded in the New Testament accounts. Here it was the custom for the father of the family to take unleavened bread in his hands, and to say this prayer "Blessed art Thou, who bringest forth bread from the earth". Then the father broke the bread in pieces. But what Jesus did was to say, "Take, eat, this is my body."

Then followed the meal proper – the eating of the Passover Lamb and the side-dishes, which, together with the prayers which followed it, might take a quarter of an hour. At the end of this course, the father of the family would normally say a prayer of thanksgiving for the meal, over a third cup of wine, called the cup of thanksgiving. But here Jesus made his second change from the customary ritual. He said, "This is my blood, which is poured out for many," or "This cup is the new covenant in my blood."

From these words and actions we may infer that he was instituting a new Covenant Feast which for his followers would take the place of the Passover Feast – though this claim would not be understood by them till some time afterwards. But when these things were understood, then the disciples saw that Christ's actions and words could bear only this meaning. They meant that he was claiming for himself and his work a centrality in the history of God's people. What he was now doing was on a par with the institution of that Passover Feast and Covenant through which the Hebrew people had long ago come into existence as a nation under God's hand.

To men of our western tradition Jesus' words "This

is my body" and "This is my blood" have a strangeness that they would not have for anyone familiar with the rite of the Passover Feast. His action and words over bread and wine are parallel with the Passover actions and interpretations. By both, he declares that his body will be broken and his blood shed.

But there is more than symbol here, for the bread and wine are *given* and *received*. The act of giving the bread and wine to the disciples to eat and drink means that this sacrifice will be for them. By their obedient eating and drinking they not only accept what he is doing for them, but appropriate it for themselves. Of this appropriation I shall have more to say in the next chapter.

This enacted parable has thus an unmistakable meaning, and Jesus also makes an unmistakable reference to the New Covenant spoken of in *Jeremiah* 31, v. 31 – a New Covenant which would replace the former Covenant which God had made with his people in Old Testament days:

"But this shall be the covenant that I will make with the house of Israel: after those days, saith the Lord, I will put my law in their inward parts, and write it in their hearts, and will be their God, and they shall be my people, for they shall all know me, from the least of them unto the greatest of them . . . for I will forgive their iniquity and I will remember their sin no more."

It is easy for sceptical critics to say that certain of Jesus' reported words are not genuine, but fall into the category of "prophecies after the event". It seems much harder to explain away the significance of this action of his, for which the historical evidence is, as we have seen, so strong. It would appear that in this action are implicit the claims which the Church has been accustomed to make for Jesus through the ages. In this action he claims to set up on the earth among men a Covenant of forgiveness which creates a new relationship of intimate fellowship between God and man, and between man and his neighbour. And it is linked with his imminent death.

Such were the actions of Jesus in Jerusalem on that night two thousand years ago, and such are the actions that we are bidden to perform when we meet together as a memorial of him. At this point interpretations vary. Men ask "Is it a memorial for ourselves, or before men, merely, or is it also a memorial before God?" "Is the aim of this rite only to bring Christ's life and death before us so that we may be grateful for it, or is there any sense in which we can be said to bring it to the memory of God?" We shall have to discuss these questions at a later time, but we may now concentrate our attention on one point, on which all Christians are agreed. These solemn and repeated acts of obedience are intended to awaken us to thankful remembrance, and it is of this act, and how we may perform it, that I wish now to speak in the closing pages of this chapter.

Let us pause for a moment to reflect how here, in the act of remembering, is struck one of the fundamental chords of our common humanity. Is it not one of the supreme characteristics that make man human, that he should remember? Not merely that he should recall, but that he should remember with gratitude and loyalty the great gifts that have come to him in his life? Taken first

at a purely human level, does it not touch us deeply when
we hear such words as these:

> What care I though all forget thee,
> I will love thee evermore.[1]

or again,

> Thine I am, and thine I shall be ever,
> When I'm in the deep grave laid![2]

To forget love, to forget those who have loved us, is to
be less than human; worse, it is to be inhuman. Forgetfulness is ingratitude, to man, and finally, to God, who is the
giver behind all human gifts.

There is a theme running through the Old Testament
to which I wish now to draw your attention. We have seen
it in the context of the Passover, but it is not present only
there. God in his kindness does great acts of mercy to his
people. Israel has done nothing whatever to deserve them.
Then he appeals to his people by the memory of these
things he has done, to encourage them to trust him for the
present and the future. He appeals in this way to them in
order to make it easier for them to trust him. We have
only to look through the *Psalms* and through the books
of *Deuteronomy* and *Isaiah* to see how central to the Bible
this pattern is.

This is a pattern of remembering, both on God's side,
and on Israel's. God remembers his people, he pleads with
them in their turn to remember him. When the Bible

[1] *Songs of the North*, MacLeod & Boulton, No. XXXVII "O'er
the Moor".

[2] Hungarian song, which I have been unable to identify.

says God remembers his people, it does not think of a vague ineffective thought passing through his mind. It means that God *acts*. He puts out his hand to save them. Then later he asks them to remember what he has done. Not because he has a petulant and small-minded desire for their adulation, but because he is their Father, and loves them. He wishes them to love him and trust him; he knows that it will be their greatest joy and liberty if they do so. He wishes to bless them in the future, and he can only give them the fullness of his gifts if they are grateful. For God's people to forget him and his kindness is the great inhumanity, the cardinal sin. And the Passover is *the* great yearly opportunity for their remembering his mercy and renewing fellowship with him. The words of our paraphrase express exactly the mood of the worshippers at the Passover Feast:

> God of our fathers, be the God
> Of their succeeding race!

In the same way, the Lord's Supper is the great occasion when we should remember God's goodness to us and renew fellowship with him. This is why one of the chief names by which it is known is the Eucharist, which means "thanksgiving". Today we have reason to ask ourselves how it is that the great things of our faith mean so little. How little our imagination kindles at the thought of what God has done for us or at the tremendous possibilities opened by him for us in adventurous living and in prayer! But how can we expect faith and gratitude to grow strong unless we take time to live with the great things that God has done for us? There are many things in these days which make faith and prayer difficult, and some of them press upon us with a new urgency. But each age has its own special difficulties, and ours is not the first in which faith needs reinforcement by the help of God.

What we are to do in the Sacrament is this, we are to remember God's gift to us in Christ so that we may be grateful for it. Every chapter in this book will aim to develop further this theme, but here at least let me make a beginning.

I have sometimes thought to myself how it would have been if we had had no New Testament, no Jesus. Let us try to imagine that all that we know about him had become an unwritten page, and that all memory of him had been blotted out of the mind of man. Of course, if this were so, then the whole history of the world would have run so differently, that we, as we now are, would not exist! But still let us try to imagine that everything in the world were to continue as it is, with this exception, that the memory, the name, and the story of Jesus were blotted out as if it had never been. The picture of the Messiah, the expected Christ, as the Old Testament looks forward to it, would for us have become a blank, and no story about Jesus' character and his teaching, about the wonderful things he did, and his impact on men, no word of his death and his resurrection, would have broken the silence of the centuries which we now know as the years of our Lord. Then suppose that we were to come upon the Hebrew expectation of the longed-for Messiah, and were to try to imagine to ourselves how it might have been if such a one had actually appeared. What would he have been like?

I can imagine myself recalling the great men of the Old Testament, and above them all, that elusive and wonderful figure, the second Isaiah, with his burning words of encouragement and faith spoken to his people in a situation of despair. I recall his challenge to his people in exile to believe in God who would lead them to their homeland like a shepherd, caring individually for each of them, though the stars of heaven and the issues of human history were also in his hand. Had the Messiah ever come, I say to myself, he might have been someone like that, but out-topping Isaiah as much as Isaiah himself outdistances the other figures of the Old Testament among whom he stands.

And now let us return to the astonishing and given fact that in Jesus we *have* that figure among us, that we *have* that story of a life lived in complete faithfulness to the Father by one who was both our brother, and yet at the same time the final revelation of the heart of God. This is not pious invention or fairy-tale. Here at one point of human history, we have that anchor which rests on final reality; now we know what God is like, and also what men were made for.

As I turn over the Gospels, story after story, I can say to myself: This is God; and this is at the same time man's trust in God as it should be. Thank God for these foolish Sadducees with their question about life after death! Thank God for that lawyer who thought he could outwit Jesus! Not only is there superb dialectical skill in these discussions and debates, but at every point that truth of which "the depth saith, it is not in me", but which we can only have because God has stooped down in mercy to give it to us.[1]

In John's Gospel,[2] Jesus uses a magnificent though grotesque figure taken from an Old Testament story.[3] He compares himself to the ladder in Jacob's dream, which stretched from heaven to earth, and from earth to heaven, on which angels were ascending from men to God, and descending from God to men. Jesus is God's means of open access to us, and our means of open access to God. This is what has in fact happened, and the inscrutable mystery is no longer a mystery of darkness, but a mystery of excessive light. The ultimate reality has found us, and declared himself to be our Father. The best, the most wonderful news is beyond all hope and expectation true, that God in Jesus has said "yes" to mankind, "yes" to each man and woman. So when in the Anglican Communion Service the Gospel is read, it is fitting that the congregation should stand, and that at the end their response should be: "Thanks be to thee, O Lord, for this thy glorious gospel."

And it is equally fitting that in the Great Prayer, at the heart of our Communion Service, there should be intertwined the theme of gratitude for what God has done for us in all the good things of our life, but especially in Christ. This prayer has been in the Communion Service for more than sixteen hundred years, it is found in the

[1] *Job* 28, v. 14.
[2] *John* 1, v. 51.
[3] *Genesis* 28, vv. 10–12.

Liturgy of Hippolytus, used in Rome in the third century. The form of the prayer I shall quote is taken from the Church of Scotland Book of Common Order,[1] and can be found in nearly identical form in the Communion Services of many other historic churches. It comes down from the fourth century, when it could have been heard in any of the great churches of Syria.

"It is verily meet, right, and our bounden duty that we should at all times and in all places give thanks unto thee, O Holy Lord, Father Almighty, Everlasting God; who didst create the heavens and the earth and all that is therein; who didst make man in thine own image, and whose tender mercies are over all thy works.

Thee, mighty God, heavenly King, we magnify and praise. With angels and archangels and all the company of heaven, we worship and adore thy glorious name, evermore praising thee, and saying:

> Holy, Holy, Holy, Lord God of Hosts,
> Heaven and earth are full of thy glory:
> Glory be to thee, O Lord most High.

Verily holy, verily blessed, art thou, Almighty and Merciful God, who didst so love the world that thou gavest thine only-begotten Son, that whosoever believeth in him should not perish, but have everlasting life. Not as we ought, but as we are able, do we bless thee for his holy incarnation, for his perfect life upon earth, for his precious sufferings and death upon the Cross, for his glorious resurrection and ascension, for his continual intercession and rule at thy right hand, for the

[1] *B.C.O. Church of Scotland*, O.U.P. 1940, pp. 118–20.

promise of his coming again, and for his gift of the Holy Spirit.[1]

Here, as always in Christian worship, thanksgiving and memory of the past are intertwined with hope for the future. Of this hope much more will have to be said in the last chapter.

[1] *Book of Common Order of the Church of Scotland*, O.U.P. 1940, pp. 118–19.

CHAPTER II

The Presence and the Gift in the Lord's Supper

When on that night of the Passover in Jerusalem Jesus broke the hallowed sequence of the Feast with the words "Take this, this is my body", and "This is my blood of the covenant", we may be agreed that at least these words signified "This means my body", "This means my blood", "This is what is going to happen to me tomorrow". Jeremias, one of the greatest of modern New Testament scholars, says that what we have here is a twofold parable. "Jesus made the broken bread a parable of the fate of his body; the blood of the grapes a symbol of his outpoured blood. 'I go to death as the true passover sacrifice' is the meaning of Jesus' last parable."[1]

But further, by the words "This is my body", "This is my blood", Jesus describes his death as one that is going to bring deliverance to men. There can really be no doubt that Jesus at this point compared himself with the Passover Lamb, whose blood had been given to inaugurate the First Covenant long ago. So Jesus claimed that by this death of his which was to come so soon, God would

[1] *The Eucharistic Words of Jesus*, Joachim Jeremias, 3rd Edn., E.T. London 1966, p. 224.

inaugurate the New Covenant which he was about to make with his people. As the Old Testament Passover sacrifice had been the gift which in ancient days the holy and righteous God had provided, whereby he and his people were to live in peace and in covenant together, so in the new age the death of Jesus would be God's gift whereby he and men could live together at peace, and in covenant together, though he was holy, and they were sinners. It must be noted that nowhere in the Bible, whether in the Old Testament or in the New, is sacrifice regarded as a means whereby man pacifies the anger of a hostile God. From start to finish sacrifice is given by God, and it does not change his mind towards man. That he gives it is a sign of his passionate longing to be at peace with us, and to have us reconciled with himself.

And we must further note, from the Gospel of *Mark*, the wideness and generosity of this offer, for Jesus said, "This is my blood of the covenant, shed for many."[1] His death was to bring joy and peace to many, to the many. This does not necessarily mean that all are numerically included in this number, but at least the term leans in that direction.

Thus far in this chapter we have not got beyond the language of sign or symbol, language that compares and likens one thing to another. It is as if Jesus had said, "As this bread has been broken and this wine poured out, so shall my body be broken and my blood poured out for you, for mankind."

But this is not all that Jesus did. As I indicated in the first chapter, he broke the bread, and *gave it to them*. He

[1] *Mark* 14, v. 24 (*N.E.B.*).

gave them the cup to drink, and they all received it, and drank of it.

It is clear that here we have passed beyond the realm of symbol. For the bread and wine were both given and received. Could there be a more vivid and unmistakable way of saying – "This death and all its benefits are for you! Receive them in humble faith. Inasmuch as you accept and eat the bread and drink the wine in humble faith, by that very act you receive my death and its benefits for your own." And as they accepted, so they received. Here then we have not merely a symbol, but a very special kind of symbol, namely a symbol which conveys what it symbolises.

No one has given a more noble expression to this significance of Christ's actions than John Calvin – "For these are words which can never lie nor deceive – Take, eat, drink, this is my body which is broken for you: this is my blood, which is shed for the remission of sins. In bidding us take, he intimates that it is ours; in bidding us eat, he intimates that it becomes one substance with us: in affirming of his body that it was broken, and of his blood that it was shed for us, he says that both were not so much his own as ours, because he took and laid down both, not for his own advantage, but for our salvation. And we ought carefully to observe, that the chief, and almost the whole energy of the sacrament consists in these words, It is broken for you; it is shed for you."[1]

Precisely the same point is made by the Westminster Shorter Catechism, when it defines a sacrament thus: "A sacrament is a holy ordinance instituted by Christ,

[1] Calvin, *Institutes of the Christian Religion*, IV, 17, 3.

wherein, by sensible signs, Christ and the benefits of the New Covenant are represented, sealed, and applied to believers."[1]

To represent is the work of a symbol, which is a sign chosen by reason of its fitness to portray the reality for which it stands. The function of a seal is to increase men's assurance that a document or title-deed is genuine. This figure of speech (the seal) plays a bigger part in the language of the Reformers than it does in the Bible. But it is a vivid figure, that has its use. Calvin employs the illustration of a document with a decree written upon it, which has a seal appended in order to give man more assurance that the document is genuinely what it claims to be. We may enlarge his illustration by suggesting that the document is one which has inscribed upon it a royal decree – let us say a reprieve or a patent of nobility – attested by the royal seal at the bottom. The decree is the word of God, his message of love to us. A document with nothing written on it, but with the royal seal attached, would have no significance. A document with a reprieve written on it, but no seal, could well be rejected as a fraud. But a document with *both* the decree written on it, *and* the royal seal appended to it, is the most trustworthy guarantee that we can possess.

However, the *Westminster Shorter Catechism* goes on beyond the words "sign" and "seal", when it speaks of the sacraments. It says that they *apply* Christ and his benefits to believers. Through them, Christ and his benefits are actually *given* to men. What do these words, "Christ and his benefits" mean? This is a question which we must

[1] *Westminster Shorter Catechism.* Answer to Question 92.

in a moment try to answer. But first there is a comment to be made.

Up to this point in the discussion all Christians, or very nearly all, are in agreement. In the Sacrament of Communion, Christ really gives himself to those who receive in faith. The Anglo-Catholic Bishop Charles Gore,[1] living in the early twentieth century, quotes with approval the seventeenth-century Anglican theologian Richard Hooker, who noticed the fundamental agreement, and Gore quotes also another Anglican, Waterland, who said of this agreement, "It is well that Romanists and Lutherans and Greeks also, even the whole East and West, have preserved it, and yet preserve it." Hooker says that this was what Calvin taught in Geneva in Reformation days, and we could add other names to the list, those of John Knox, and, a few years after him, Robert Bruce, who was minister in St. Giles's Cathedral in Edinburgh, as well as the names of the men who wrote the Westminster Confession and Catechisms in the middle of the seventeenth century. It is a wonderful thing, a thing for which we should be grateful, that in this high and difficult question, there should be this fundamental and far-reaching agreement.

I do not mean to suggest that an account is here being given of an earlier agreement on essentials followed by a disagreement say, in a subsequent century, on subsidiary matters. I merely wish to point out that there was a basic agreement, and that it was at a point beyond this that men differed among themselves. They began to analyse the nature of Christ's presence. Their original motive was

[1] Gore, *The Body of Christ* (London), J. Murray, p. 51.

good. They were eager to maintain that Christ was really present. They wanted to safeguard a most precious truth. When the Sacrament was celebrated, men were not merely remembering an event in the dim and receding past. Christ was really and truly there. Their opponents spoke much of the need for faith in those who receive the Sacrament. Was this not to reduce Christ's presence to a mere imagination? Or again, if I cannot receive him without faith, how can I ever be sure that I have enough faith truly to receive him? My thoughts will inevitably be turned inwards to examine my own state of mind, when I ought humbly to be acknowledging the presence of the Lord.

All this was misunderstanding, but it was understandable, and the desire of the high churchmen to emphasise the real presence had led some of them to use language which on its side justly shocked those of the other party, language about chewing and swallowing Christ, which was offensive. So that the result of the controversy was unfortunately not the glory of God, nor the due adoration of the mysteriously present Lord, but mutual recrimination and persecution.

But in spite of these debates, it is today true, as it has been all along, that the great majority of Christian people are united in the belief that Christ is truly present in the Lord's Supper, and that in it, in a mysterious communion, he gives himself and his benefits to those who receive him in humble faith.

From this agreed position we can go forward to say more about the nature of the *presence* of Christ in the Sacrament, and the nature of the *gift* there given to us. These themes are allied, but not identical. In speaking of the presence, there is a special danger of defining and analysing unprofitably, where the only fitting response to that presence is one of worship. What is said here is written with this danger in mind, and in the hope that it may help the reader both to understand and at the same time to worship.

The presence of Christ in the Sacrament is the presence of the Lord: it is a living and personal presence. It is given to us in love and humility – what humility could be greater than that of him who gave himself wholly up for us? And yet he is not given into our power; he remains the Lord. But there is an assurance that he will not fail to give us his presence: it is the assurance afforded by his own promise: "This is my body, which is for you. This do ye. . . ." "Wheresoever two or three are gathered together in my name, there am I in the midst of them."[1]

Further, his presence is always a presence to faith. Without faith we cannot worthily receive him. True, even where faith is wanting, he is there, and our failure to receive him judges us. So this presence is not created by faith, or dependent on faith, much less imagined by faith.[2]

Again, the Lord who is present with us is the Risen Lord who dwells now in the mystery of the Father, exalted to the place of supreme dignity and power. Yet he is still the same Jesus, who lived for a short time wholly exposed to our human joys, and sufferings, and temptations. So, as the author to the Hebrews says, "Ours is not a high priest unable to sympathise with our weaknesses, but one who,

[1] *Matthew* 18, v. 20.
[2] D. M. Baillie, *Theology of the Sacraments* (London 1957), p. 97.

because of his likeness to us, has been tested every way, only without sin."[1] His life and his death qualify him to feel with us, his exaltation and rule qualify him to help us.

Dr. Donald Baillie has written reverent and profound words on this subject of the presence. He says that it is important to note that, even apart from the Sacrament, we are bound to distinguish several degrees or modes of the Divine Presence. To begin with the most general, we believe in the omnipresence of God. He is everywhere present.

"And yet we also say that God is with those who trust and obey him in a way in which he is not with others. We say, God is with them. And we say that God's presence is with us *more* at some times than at others. We speak of entering his presence in worship, and we ask' him to come and be with us and grant us his presence. We say that wherever two or three are gathered together in his name, he is there in the midst of them. And then in a still further sense we speak of the Real Presence in the sacrament. What does all that mean?"[2]

Baillie goes on to distinguish various senses of the word "present" as used by the philosophers, and here I would leave off quoting from his text, and sum up the drift of his argument. If we can use the word "presence" of dead objects at all – and Baillie is doubtful if we can – when we use the word of persons it does not only mean physical presence. For a person may be physically in the same room with us, and yet, as we say, "thousands of miles away from us" – more distant than someone who is

[1] *Hebrews* 4, vv. 15–16 (N.E.B.).
[2] Baillie, *Theology of the Sacraments*, pp. 97–8.

perhaps physically far away. So the notion of presence, in relation to people, surely has in it the notion of their interest, their sympathy, their will to enter into communion with us. And while our response to that presence does not create their presence with us, it allows them to make use of it, and, as it were, intensify it.

Here once again, I would take up Dr. Baillie's exact words, and quote from him. "All this reaches its climax in the sacrament of the Lord's Supper, where the God who was incarnate in Jesus uses the symbols of the sacrament as a special means of awakening the faith of his people that they may receive him, since faith is the channel by which God's most intimate presence comes to men in this earthly life."[1]

This is surely in agreement with the Scottish Confession of Faith, written in 1560. Here the Confession is speaking of the life and immortality which are given to believing partakers of the Sacrament. Referring to these gifts, it says, "Quhilk, albeit we confesse are nether given unto us at that time onelie, nether zit be the proper power and vertue of the Sacrament onelie; zit we affirme that the faithfull, in the richt use of the Lord's Table, hes conjunction with Christ Jesus as the naturall man cannot apprehend."[2]

Now we come to a point where it is hard to find agreement among Christians. There are those who maintain that there is no difference between the presence of Christ wherever men worship him in faith, and his presence in the Lord's Supper. The Scottish Confession, as we saw,

[1] *Ibid*, p. 99.
[2] *Confessio Scoticana*, Article XXI.

does not commit itself on that point. Certainly it would be wrong to define the presence in the Supper in such a way as to suggest that Christ is not really present wherever prayer is made in his name, and Christian faith calls upon God through him. It is possible that even to ask whether there is such a distinction in his presence as this is to engage in an idle and irreverent speculation. But surely we can nearly all be agreed, as Christians, that in the Lord's Supper, in a quite singular way, through physical actions, believers appropriate the gift which he has to give, and this is all we need to know. But with this we have passed from the theme of the *presence* of the Lord in the sacramental act, to the *gift* given in it, and here we are on safer ground, where we are less likely to get involved in idle speculations that would inevitably lead to triviality and dissension rather than to worship and harmony.

Twenty years after the publication of Knox's Scottish Confession, Mr. Robert Bruce, the Minister of St. Giles's in Edinburgh, spoke the following words in one of his famous sermons on the Sacraments, comparing the gift given in the Sacrament with that given in the preaching of the Word. I make no excuse for quoting him rather fully.

"We admit that . . . we get no other thing, nor no new thing in the Sacrament, but the same thing which we got in the word. I would have thee devise and imagine with thyself, what new thing thou wouldst have; let the heart of man devise, imagine, and wish, he durst never have thought to have such a thing as the Son of God; he durst never have presumed, to have pierced the clouds, to have ascended so high, to have craved the Son of God in his flesh to be the food of his soul . . . Having the Son of

God, thou hast him who is the heir of all things, who is King of Heaven and earth; and in him thou hast all things. What more canst thou wish? . . .

But suppose it to be so; yet the Sacrament is not superfluous. Suppose thou gets that same thing which thou hadst in the word, yet thou gettest that same thing better . . . he has larger bounds in thy soul by the receiving of the sacrament, than otherwise he could have by the hearing of the word only. . . . For by the Sacrament my faith is nourished, the bounds of my soul are enlarged; and so, whereas I had but a little hold of Christ before, as it were, between my finger and thumb, now I get him in my whole hand, and still the more that my faith grows, the better hold I get of Christ Jesus."[1]

Here, obviously, Bruce is using a physical metaphor which cannot be taken in its literal sense – "hand" and 'finger and thumb" and "larger bounds in thy soul" are the terms used. But these terms help us to "grasp" the meaning better. And the Sacrament itself, by its divinely appointed use of physical things both to symbolise and convey spiritual realities, is similarly fitted to perform its special work.

But what do the terms which we have been using mean? What, in particular, do we mean when we speak of "Christ and his benefits"? What is meant when we talk about these being "applied" to believers? This is language which we must try to restate in such a way that it means something for twentieth-century believers.

Of course there is mystery here. That is why there are so many different figures of speech used in the New

[1] *Robert Bruce's Sermons on the Sacrament*; Edinburgh 1901, p. 63.

Testament to describe this relationship of believers to Christ. None of them can be meant quite literally; all are necessary as pointing to the ineffable reality.

The Fourth Gospel uses consciously shocking language when it describes believers as eating the flesh of Christ and drinking his blood. A few chapters later it uses another figure, that of the branches drawing life and vigour from the parent vine. And St. Paul can say that Christ is in his followers, or that they are in him. Clearly, here, in dramatic eastern language, something is being said about the deep and mysterious bond between Christ and his Church, and between him and individual Christians, which it is safe to say that we shall never fully understand, though we can experience it more and more fully. And indeed, looking back, we can say that now we both experience it and understand it much more fully than once we did.

We may ask whether it is possible to distinguish between the gift of Christ's benefits, and the gift of himself. We have only to reflect in order to see that the answer must be "No". Another person may give us benefits without giving us himself, but in the case of Christ, we can see that such an abstraction is impossible. And yet the gift of himself more than sums up the list of benefits which he gives for these are but the expressions of his love suited to our varying needs, and in all of them he gives us himself.

As Dr. Adamson says, "It will always be natural that every man's view of the rite should be vitally coloured by his distinctive apprehension of the Gospel. Yet, we would contend, no catalogue of special blessings received can suffice to express the fullness of the gift offered in the Holy Supper. The nature of the greatness of that gift can be expressed only by saying that it consists of Christ himself".[1]

Adamson claims that the gift of the body and the blood signifies the gift of Christ's whole personality. He points out that, though here we are in the presence of a mystery, yet the analogy of ordinary human relationships can start us up the way of understanding. "In ordinary life," he says, "the power of a good and strong personality is distinctly felt by others to be a positive contribution to their spiritual capital. Virtue goes out from the stronger to the weaker. Even here it is clear that something infinitely richer is under consideration than the mere power of a good example. We have all known men and women who have so given themselves to us that we might almost say that we owe everything to them." Adamson does not, of course, stop here, but goes on to describe in his own manner the fuller and particular character of the gift in the Christian sacrament.

Here we may leave him, and ask, taking our own independent line of thought, "What does it mean that Christ gives himself to us?" Here the whole of the salvation which he brings, and the whole doctrine of atonement is implied. But in a word, we can say that he gives himself to us as our Saviour. One of the insights which, though not new, have been enormously deepened and brought into focus by the work of the psychotherapists, has been this, that it is only love, given to the growing

[1] Adamson, *Christian Doctrine of the Lord's Supper*. Edinburgh 1905, pp. 153–4.

child, which can provide for him the security that will enable him to transcend his own aggression, his self-seeking and his fear, and enable him to love in return. Here we have a certain secular confirmation of the belief that the fundamental nature of man is to love, and that failures in love are aberrations from this true humanity. Now where man realises that *God* himself loves him in spite of all his weakness and perversity, this, if truly taken home, begins to restore him to his true humanity. Jesus brings to us that forgiveness which only God can give; he restores to us our lost sonship of God, and sets free our power to love other people. He does for us what only our kinsman Redeemer can do. He commits himself irrevocably to us as friend, master, companion, in life and death, and beyond it. Not only does he remove the alienation between us and the Father caused by our sin, but he stands surety to the Father and to us that we shall yet be all that the Father requires us to be.

In this giving of himself, renewed in the Sacrament, he stands before us as the One who has offered himself for us, and opened to us the doorway of new life. In this giving of himself, there is no kind of infusion such as would blur the distinction between us and God. We are not fused with God, nor do we become one substance with him as the Hindu imagines:

The dewdrop slips into the shining sea.

What happens is that we are restored to that relationship with the Father, which the Father planned for us from the beginning. We are made sons in the Father's family, and in the Father's house, with all the privileges of sons. I once heard a Highland preacher say "There is no turn of the stairs in the Father's house, which Jesus does not know". This is true, and he gives to us the same intimacy of sonship, and the same freedom there which he has, as man.

Without irreverence a further thought might be added here, only to be welcomed by the reader if it brings light to him. Our human nature is not a kind of special fluid or substance in us, but is constituted by this, that we all of us, in every thought, action, and decision, are constantly responding to the creative word of God. This continual presence before him, responsible to him, and responding to him, is apparently not shared by any other living being of which we have knowledge. This it is, which makes us responsible beings, and this is true, even of those who do not believe in God, as it is of those who are in conscious rebellion against him. If this be true, then he who does for us what God alone can do, who restores us to the right relationship with the Father, gives us the power to make the right response. And by that act he restores to us our true humanity, our true sonship, so that we can love and trust and obey our Father. This restoration is given to us, or confirmed to us when we partake of the Sacrament in faith, and there is no reason why every part of our being should not in some degree participate in its life-giving effects.

Christ also in the Sacrament opens the way for a renewal of the right relationship between us and other men, if we accept his gift in faith and obedience. Until Jesus came we never knew clearly – nor indeed could we know – what true human nature is. Jesus has been well described as "the man for other men". Now in him we see the true humanity, and the door to it is wide open to us through his gift. We, too, must be men for other men. By being for us he sets us free to enter into our true humanity. Therefore all that sonship of the Father which as man he possessed, the same confidence, the same deep joy and peace, the same calm beneath all surface distresses, the same thought for others; all these are included in the gift of the supper, and what could be higher or more splendid?

It is as if we stood on a radiant summer morning at an open door, with the trees and flowers outside lying still under the rising sun. We are free to step forth into the beauty around us, to enter upon the humanity given to us by Christ.

> Deck thyself, my soul, with gladness,
> Leave the gloomy haunts of sadness,
> Come into the daylight's splendour,
> There with joy thy praises render
> Unto Him whose grace unbounded
> Hath this wondrous banquet founded,
> High o'er all the heavens He reigneth,
> Yet to dwell with thee He deigneth.[1]

[1] *Church Hymnary*, 324, Hymn by Johann Franck.

CHAPTER III

Fellowship in the Lord's Supper

A Swiss writer has recently brought to our attention the strange fact that the Bible ends, as it began, with a story about eating.[1] In *Genesis* the fact of man's fall away from God is symbolised by the tale of the woman eating fruit in the garden, while at the end of the *Book of Revelation* there is the story of the marriage supper of the Lamb. And this depicts in a symbolic manner the return of humanity after the long epic of history to the welcome and the feast in the Father's house. Not only so, but in the middle of the Bible we have the picture of him whom his enemies called a glutton and a wine-bibber seated at table. He breaks the bread, and says, "Take, eat."

Eating and drinking together at table is one of the great central human symbols. It is, indeed, more than a symbol of fellowship; it creates fellowship between the host and those who sit with him at his table, and it binds them also to one another.

We saw already how in the Old Testament the Passover was not only a sacrifice, but also a feast. It was looked on as a solemn yearly renewal of God's Covenant with his people. And it united the guests with each other in a wonderful fellowship, as they looked back on the mighty

[1] Rudolf Bohren.

memories which bound them to God and to each other as a people.

There can be no doubt that the same senses of close fellowship with Christ and with each other was a central theme of the Lord's Supper in the early Church. It was so from the very start. Let us look first at the narrative concerning the Last Supper. When Jesus sat down with the twelve in the Upper Room, "he had always loved them, and now he was to show the full extent of his love".[1] He saw, too, how great was their danger. He washed their feet to show his love to them, and to give them an example of the love they were to show one another. Only in his love and in love for each other would they be safe.

Putting together what Luke tells us, with what John tells us, we can infer that the lamentable dispute about priority of which Luke speaks, was the occasion for the foot-washing incident which only John records. And Luke adds Jesus' words "among you there must be no search for pre-eminence, but the greatest must be the servant of all, for I myself am among you as a servant".

Almost immediately afterwards, he gave his warning to Peter, "Simon, Simon, take heed, Satan has been given leave to sift all of you like wheat, but I have prayed for you, that your faith may not fail, and when you have come to yourself, you must lend strength to your brothers."[2]

From all this we see how intensely Jesus desired that his disciples should remain in fellowship, should stand

[1] *John* 13, v. 1., *N.E.B.*
[2] *Luke* 22, vv. 31–33, *N.E.B.*

fast against the terrible temptation that threatened to destroy the Church at the very outset of its life, and has threatened it ever since. If only through the ages the Church had heeded that warning! If only it could take it more to heart now!

Sometimes the very familiarity of a thing makes us unable to appreciate it. Then there are ways by which we can restore its freshness, so that we can come upon it as if it were a new discovery. Let us suppose that tomorrow we were to open our newspapers and to find that a remarkable new scroll had been found in a cave above the Dead Sea. As the weeks passed, it became more and more clear that what the searchers had unearthed was nothing less than the meditation of our Lord spoken to his disciples at the table in the upper room on the night before he died. With what eagerness and wonder we would seize upon this discovery, how avidly we would scan it, and appreciate its priceless value!

Yet it is in fact widely agreed that we do possess the substance of that meditation in the 14th to the 17th chapters of *St. John*, chapters which are among the greatest in the whole New Testament. Are they not, in a sense, self-authenticating? Are they not worthy of that occasion? Who could have invented them? Could they have come from anyone but Jesus?

Here the theme is that of his followers abiding in him as the branches abide in the vine, of loving him and each other, as the Father has loved him, and as Jesus has loved them. For he has kept back nothing of what the Father has told him, but imparted it to them. And now he is going to his death for them. Greater love hath no man than this, that a man lay down his life for his friends. The whole of these four chapters, including the prayer in which they culminate, is one majestic development of this theme; the unity of love and mutual confidence which binds together the Father and the Son, a door which is thrown wide open to admit the fellowship of the disciples and all those who through them will believe in Jesus' name. "O righteous Father, the world hath not known thee, but I have known thee, and these have known that thou hast sent me. And I have declared unto them thy name, and will declare it, that the love wherewith thou has loved me may be in them, and I in them."[1]

Now let us look at the Gospel story in its earlier stages, and we shall find ourselves led to the same conclusion. Modern New Testament scholarship has opened to us the most fascinating new lines of thought on this theme of fellowship in the Sacrament, particularly in relation to this earlier part of the Gospel story. There are some points on which the scholars are still not agreed, but on some there is a substantial agreement, and it is these which must be considered now.

It is now generally agreed that the sacramental meal which came into existence in the early Church did not owe its origin solely to the Passover Supper which Jesus took with his disciples on the night of his betrayal. In all probability Jesus had been eating meals of a special character through the days of his public ministry, not only with the inner circle of his disciples, but with larger groups of men and women – including people of questionable character and notorious sinners. It is at least

[1] *John* 17, vv. 25–26 (*A.V.*).

48

possible that the stories preserved in the Gospels of the miraculous feeding of the crowds, took their origin in such meals, and that, for another example, the meal in the house of Zacchaeus had this special character. You will remember that Jesus invited himself to dinner at Zacchaeus's house. (*Luke* 19, v. 5).

This eating with sinners was a spontaneous act of love, but it had also a further meaning. To liken a greater thing to a lesser, though still important one, it was like white people sitting publicly down to dine together with coloured people in a segregated society. It was a sign that the old barriers were down, and that the old hatreds and restrictions were no longer in force. Further, there was in it the dimension of depth; it was a visible symbol of the forgiveness of God which was proclaimed in the words of Jesus. It was, like his healings, a sign that God's Kingdom was at hand, was even now breaking in.

Further, it was generally understood that when the Messiah came, he would heal the sick, and would share a feast with his people. These feasts, like Jesus' cleansing of the Temple Court, were silent claims that he who did these things was no ordinary man. An era had come to its end, and a new age had dawned, the age of the Kingdom of God.

It is probable that the intense resentment caused by Jesus eating with publicans and sinners, arose not merely because the Pharisees hated to see him mixing with such people, but because they perceived the claim underlying these actions of his. His eating with these people was a dramatic way of claiming to forgive their sins, to bring God's presence among them.

Jeremias has made an interesting observation. He points out that, after Jesus' confession at Caesarea Philippi that he was the Christ, no meal that the disciples ate with him henceforth could be the same as before.[1] They would look on every meal to which they sat down with him as pointing towards the Messianic banquet at the end of the age.

This banquet was always thought of as a feast of fellowship and reconciliation. So it had been in Old Testament prophecy. Had not Isaiah painted it in glowing language – "And in this mountain shall the Lord of hosts make unto all people a feast of fat things . . . and he will destroy in this mountain the face of the covering cast over all people, and the veil that is spread over all nations, he will swallow up death in victory."[2]

Again, in the parable of the Prodigal Son, Jesus spoke of a feast of rejoicing and reconciliation to which the father receives the prodigal – as he would gladly also receive the elder brother. Perhaps it was at one of the meals to which he received sinners that Jesus spoke this parable. Be this as it may, these feasts of welcome surely foreshadowed the great final feast of which Jesus spoke when he told of men at the last coming in from the east and the west and sitting down together in the Kingdom of God.

The point which I have been making is this, that not only the Last Supper was intended by Jesus to be a feast of fellowship, but the feasts which led up to it clearly had this character too. It may be that they were feasts open

[1] Jeremias, *The Eucharistic Words of Jesus*, 3rd edition, p. 205.
[2] *Isaiah* 25, vv. 6–7.

to anyone, while there is no evidence that the Sacrament was given beyond the circle of believers. But the keynote was the same; here were feasts that meant the breaking down of barriers between God and man, and between man and his brother man.

If we now leave the story of what happened during Jesus' lifetime, and turn to the stories of his appearances after his resurrection, we find a surprising number of references to the fact that he ate and drank with them on these occasions.

We have the story of the Emmaus inn, though here, to be exact, it was as he broke the bread, before the meal had actually begun, that he vanished from them. Then there was the occasion which immediately followed this, on the return of those two disciples to Jerusalem, when he appeared to the twelve, and ate and drank with them. There is the story of the fourth Gospel, where he is reported to have breakfasted with them by the lakeside, and there are the words of Peter to Cornelius in *Acts*, "God raised him to life on the third day, and allowed him to appear, not to the whole people, but to witnesses whom God had chosen in advance, who ate and drank with him after he rose from the dead."[1]

Now it is true that at this distance of time, and from the accounts that we possess, it is no longer possible to construct a coherent scheme into which we can fit the various resurrection appearances, but one thing is clear, this association of the risen Lord with the act of eating and drinking with disciples. Cullmann says that the intense joy of the primitive Church sacraments, which is

[1] *Acts* 10, vv. 40-1.

recorded in *Acts* 2, v. 42, was due to the conviction, that when the Christians broke bread together, the Lord, though invisible, was with them. He was just as truly there as the host and giver of the feast, as he had been at those meals just after the resurrection, when they could see him. It may well be that Jesus' own words, recorded in the gospels, "Wheresoever two or three are gathered together in my name, there I am in the midst of them"[1] was a word which found its chief, though not its only, fulfilment on those occasions when they broke bread together in his name. Their love to each other found its principal expressions and guarantee on the occasion when together they gathered round his table.

Finally, we must add the testimony of Paul in his first letter to the Corinthians. Here he is confronted with an abuse of the Lord's Supper by the people to whom he is writing. There has been dissension and disorder among them, such disorder that some have been turned away hungry from the love feast, while others have been sated and drunken. Faced by this appalling failure to see the real significance of the Sacrament, Paul tells them in solemn language how Jesus instituted this Sacrament of his death on their behalf.[2]

There are different ways of interpreting Paul's exact meaning here, but there can be no doubt of his central concern. He is urging the Corinthians to remember that they eat from one loaf at Christ's table. This is a symbol of their belonging together to one Christ in one body, the Church. By eating in faith they are actually made one

[1] *Matthew* 18, v. 5.
[2] 1 *Corinthians* 11, vv. 17–34.

with him and with each other. If they understand this so little as to have contentions and disputes for priority among themselves, then they are eating and drinking judgement to themselves.

Our conclusion is thus four times reinforced; first from the narrative about the institution of the Lord's Supper; second, from the nature of the feasts shared by Jesus with sinners in the earlier part of his ministry; third, by the character of the meals shared by the disciples with the risen Lord, and fourth, by the nature of the Communion in the primitive Church, as borne witness to by St. Paul and the book of *Acts*.

Now, if all this be true, how can it have come to pass that this theme of fellowship plays so small a part in our religious and sacramental teaching? How can it possibly have come about that in all the dozens of books written by authors of all denominations about the Sacrament, there is so little about the theme of fellowship, when every other aspect has received the closest attention, and examination, often to no edification either of the unbelieving world or the believing Church?

How can men choose rather to debate among themselves such questions as "Do the faithful chew Christ's body with their teeth?" or "How can the body of Christ be upon our altars when it is distant in heaven?" "Is Christ given in the Sacrament to unbelievers, or only to those who receive him in faith?" These questions and others like them have been debated in such a manner as to destroy fellowship, while too often the theme of fellowship and the thing itself have been forgotten.

Is it not shameful that we have taken that very

Sacrament which Christ gave to us as the safeguard of unity, and have made of it the bitterest cause of division and contention? There is not in our Church Hymnary one hymn worth singing which honestly confesses the shame and scandal of our sacramental disunity, and prays that it may be overcome. It is not until this twentieth century, and this last year that such a hymn has been written:

> Lord Christ, the Father's mighty Son,
> Whose work upon the Cross was done,
> All men to receive,
> Make all our scattered churches one,
> That the world may believe.
>
> To make us one your prayers were said.
> To make us one you broke the bread,
> Its pieces scattered us instead,
> How can others believe?
>
> O Christ, forgive us, make us new!
> We know the best that we can do
> Will nothing achieve,
> And, humbled, bring our prayers to you
> That the world may believe.
>
> We will not question or refuse,
> The way you work, the means you choose,
> The pattern you weave,
> But reconcile our warring views,
> That the world may believe.[1]

[1] Brian Wren, *Dunblane Hymns* I, obtainable from the Warden, Scottish Churches' House, Dunblane.

In theory, indeed, we of the Presbyterian Communion have even less reason than others for neglecting this aspect of fellowship. For we do not speak of an altar, but of the Lord's Table, the symbol of fellowship, divine and human. In our Churches this table is not remote from the people, faced by a celebrant whose back is turned to the congregation. The minister, surrounded by the elders, facing the congregation, should in every way remind the worshippers of the Lord, turned towards his people in grace, who is himself the giver of the feast.

And the participation of the elders and the worshippers, who pass the bread and the wine from hand to hand, should continually remind us that it is not only the Lord himself who gives to each member of the family, but that he does it through our neighbour's giving and fellowship.

It would not be profitable to try to diagnose the reasons for this lack of vision in the Christian Churches. Doubtless there may be parts of the Church where sacramental fellowship has received a more worthy emphasis than others. It is more relevant that we should consider how we may restore it to its rightful place. And for us now the best way may be to make an indirect approach to the theme.

I remember, many years ago, hearing the early Church described as a series of groups of friends in seaports and towns and remote villages throughout the Mediterranean world, each one gathered round the invisible Christ. Let us suppose that at our worship one Sunday, the same thing were to happen as happened in the upper room on the night after the walk to Emmaus. Suppose

that Christ himself were to appear in our midst and talk
to us. There would be many things that he would say to
us; some who were troubled and anxious would hear
from him words of encouragement for which they had
never dared to hope, and words of praise they never
expected to hear. There would also be things that he had
to say to us, searching and healing to our individual
consciences.

But certainly there would be many things concerning
our corporate life and fellowship, which would open our
eyes to see each other with a new charity and tenderness,
so that instead of passing chilly and trivial judgements
upon each other we would be driven to acts of kindness
and sympathy we had not dreamt of.

There would be things told us about needs in our parish
and our city which, corporately or individually, we had
never seen before, about new ventures to be undertaken
in the secular world, new ventures of friendship to
Christians separated from us by differences of faith. Our
eyes would be opened to the needs of young people, old
people, and the disinherited and hungry nations. Would
not the total result be a great turning away of our attention from ourselves and the Gospel as a comfort to us, to
the Gospel as a gift to the world? Christ would tell us
how often he had looked for intercessors, and had found
none. Would he not say "When God has done so much
for you, how do you thank him so little? And why do
you not go on to ask for what he longs to give to those
who intercede with him in my name. Little children,
love one another, serve one another, then the glory which
the Father gave to me I will give to you, that you may be

one, even as the Father and I are one, and the world may know that he has sent me."

A Church that is thus united with the Son and the Father will not remain self-centred, but will be guided by the Spirit, and will reveal God's glory to the world. Is it because of this self-centred individualism, this lack of obedience, that we have lost our unity?

There is another fellowship in the Sacrament of which the New Testament says something, though not much. It would therefore be fitting to say something, though not much, about it here. It is not mentioned in the New Testament in the explicit context of the Sacrament. Yet, as we shall see, the Sacrament looks forward to the final hope, the consummation of God's purposes – and in that context we cannot but think of our fellowship with those who have loved Christ and who are now with him, and whom we hope to see again.

Saint Paul mentions this hope in the first letter to the Thessalonians,[1] and recalling the necessary inadequacy of his language, as of all language, to describe his meaning, I may quote his words now – "We want you not to remain in ignorance, brothers, about those who sleep in death. You should not grieve like the rest of men who have no hope. We believe that Jesus died and rose again, and so it will be for those who died as Christians, God will bring them in company with Jesus."

I understand this as follows – This use of the word *sleep* is not to be taken as literally meaning that they are unconscious. Nor can the picture be taken literally as implying a physical return of Christ and the blessed dead to this

[1] 1 *Thessalonians* 4, vv. 13–14.

earth, for in that case the inexpressible and transcendent nature of the event would be lost. They are with Christ in the Father's nearer presence, and when the barriers between time and eternity are transcended, when we meet with him, we shall also meet with them. We have true communion with him now, though we do not see him. As we have communion with him, so do we have fellowship with them in our relationship to him, and this fellowship should be felt with peculiar strength in the hour of sacramental worship. As we belong to him for ever, so do we belong to them.

And in the Lord's Supper we should be specially aware of the cloud of witnesses who surround us, who in company with us will reach their full perfection when God's purposes with mankind are complete. There are among them the great names, and the humble ones, and particularly we feel close to those who loved us and love us still.

It may or may not be right for us to pray for them, it is certainly right for us to thank God for them, to remember them with love, and we may be sure that they are interceding for us. Therefore it is fitting that in our Communion Service there should be a place for them, especially at the beginning and at the end.

Near the beginning, at the end of the Intercession Prayer, we pray thus – Eternal God, with whom are the issues of life, we give thee thanks for all thy saints who, having in this life witnessed a good confession, have left the light of their example to shine before thy people; especially those beloved by us who are now with thee. Bring us into communion with them here in thy holy presence; and enable us so to follow them in all godly living, that hereafter we may with them behold thy face in glory, and in the heavenly places be one with them for ever.[1]

And the second part of the final prayer from the Communion Service runs as follows:

And rejoicing in the communion of saints, we thank and praise thee for all thy servants who have departed in the faith, the great cloud of witnesses by whom we are compassed about; all thy saints in every age who have loved thee in life and continued faithful unto death; especially those dear to our own hearts. . . . Give us grace to follow them as they followed Christ; and bring us with them, at the last, to those things which eye hath not seen, nor ear heard, which thou hast prepared for them that love thee, through Jesus Christ our Lord, who liveth and reigneth, and is worshipped and glorified, with thee, O Father, and the Holy Spirit, world without end. Amen.[2]

[1] *Book of Common Order*, p. 115.
[2] *Book of Common Order*, p. 122.

CHAPTER IV

Sacrifice and Intercession in the Lord's Supper

Here we come upon a theme which has been most bitterly disputed, and the words "the sacrifice of the Mass" can still waken animosity among people who might be hard put to it to explain what they mean!

In the 29th Article of the Westminster Confession we read – "In this sacrament Christ is not offered up to his Father, nor any real sacrifice made at all for remission of sins of the quick or dead, but only a commemoration of that one offering up of himself, by himself, upon the cross once for all and a spiritual oblation of all possible praise unto God for the same, so that the Popish sacrifice of the mass, as they call it, is most abominably injurious to Christ's one only sacrifice, the alone propitiation for all the sins of the elect."

Perhaps at this point the simple believer, or would-be believer, is tempted to cry "a plague of both your houses!" "How can you," he asks, "still be debating whether in the Lord's Supper we offer up Christ's sacrifice to God, or whether, on the other hand, what we offer to him is merely the gratitude of our hearts and the dedication of our wills in his service? In a world where most men regard the whole Christian faith as an outworn super-

stition, where even believers find the very notion of
sacrifice every year more remote and unintelligible, how
can you continue with this wearisome debate, so far away
from the world's need, so inimical to the spirit of worship
itself?

It certainly does seem that there are refinements of the
discussion on the Sacrament which have no value for
life or worship, and which can therefore be omitted
from such a book as this, and which might well be quietly
dropped even from technical theological discussion.

Yet it is necessary to say something here on this subject
of sacrifice in the Lord's Supper. And that for two
reasons. First, there has been much misunderstanding
which can only be cleared up by patient conversation
between the Churches. This is in full course at the
moment, and I would like to add my small contribution
to it.

And, second, I believe that there is an issue of fundamental importance at stake in the debate, an issue which
justified the decisiveness, perhaps even some of the bitter-
ness with which the Reformers repudiated the teaching
of the contemporary Roman Church on the sacrifice of
the Mass.

Luther protested against the theory and practice of the
Roman Church in his day, because, as he claimed, it
turned the Gospel upside down. What is the essence of
the Gospel? – That when man cannot put himself right
with God, God has taken the initiative and in Christ has
done all that was necessary. Christ offered himself for this
great purpose of God. "He went the way of sacrifice in
obedience to his heavenly Father." For sacrifice is essentially

this, a costly means given by God whereby he, the God of holiness and righteousness, and sinful men can live together in peace. Christ has finished the atonement, the victory has been won, the sacrifice is fulfilled and valid for ever.

This sacrifice is perfect and complete in God's eyes, no addition to it is either necessary or possible. To attempt to add to it in any way is to deny that Christ's act of atonement and sacrifice is sufficient and valid for ever. Behind the doctrine of the sacrifice of the Mass, as Luther confronted it in the Roman Church of his day, there lurks the conception that even after Christ's act of atonement, God remains the unreconciled God, who must be appeased by continued sacrifices.[1]

One of the most interesting and hopeful signs of the times in the relationships of the Churches is this, that Roman Catholic and High Anglican writers have not been uninfluenced by this criticism, and have in varying ways tried to reformulate their doctrines of the sacrifice of the Mass, drawing also upon other strands in the tradition of their own Churches. Perhaps these reformulations imply a measure of acknowledgement that the criticism was, in part at least, just. To follow these new developments here would be both impossible and unfitting to the purpose of this book.

It would be much more relevant to the purpose in hand if we were to make a very brief study of the New Testament teaching about Christ's work as a priest. What is fitting for me to do, is to draw on some of the Biblical

[1] c.f. Aulen, *Eucharist and Sacrifice*, E. T. Oliver & Boyd, Edinburgh 1958, pp. 83–84. The gist of the argument is given here.

teaching about Christ's work, as I understand it. The book in the Bible which has by far the most important contribution to make on this subject is the letter to the Hebrews. The unknown writer of this letter sees Jesus' work as the sacrifice of a priest. He is probably writing to Hebrew Christians tempted to fall back into the old Jewish ways of religion, through fear of suffering persecution for the new Christian faith. He is therefore writing to men and women to whom this whole language and thought about priesthood and sacrifice was familiar as it is not to us.

But at this point we modern men and women are faced by several difficulties. For we are very tempted to ask ourselves, why should we, nearly two thousand years after the destruction of the temple and altar in Jerusalem, be forced to think in these terms? Is not that whole world of thought nothing better than Jewish old clothes, as Carlyle once described it?

To that argument we must give this answer. We believe if we are Christians, that there was a real approach of God to the men of Israel in the revelation of the Old Testament. And the coming of Jesus *to them* was not an accident. Therefore the ways of thinking of that old nation, and its religious practices, were not utterly irrelevant to God's fuller purpose. Christ's coming certainly made their institutions and their concepts out of date. But he and the revelation which came with him brought also the *fulfilment* of what was central and highest in the old religion. Therefore, to use the thoughts of priesthood and sacrifice to describe what he has done for mankind, is one legitimate and, indeed, necessary way of understanding what he has done, though it is not the only way. Now this attempt to interpret what Jesus has done as the fulfilment of all that was central and highest in the Old Testament religion, is precisely what the author to the Hebrews has set before us. For his main argument is "Do not go back to Judaism, because Christ's priesthood and Christ's sacrifice is as much superior to the priesthood and the sacrifices of the Old Testament, as the New Covenant of God with man is more glorious than the old one!"

So though we today are under no temptation to go back literally to the Jewish religion, yet the writing in Hebrews can throw a light upon Jesus and what he has done for us that we can in no other way receive.

A second difficulty is perhaps even more urgent in these days when we have become so conscious of the inadequacy of all language when it is applied to the mysteries of divine things. Is the inadequacy not so extreme in this particular context as to imply a complete breakdown into nonsense? Is it not incredibly naïve to discuss whether in Hebrews Christ is imagined as standing or sitting at God's right hand, whether he is pictured as continually offering his sacrifice, or else as interceding on the basis of a sacrifice once for all, long ago, offered and accepted? And some may go on to ask whether the very notion of Christ interceding with the Father for us is not an intolerable one, on moral grounds, since it assumes that the Father is hostile to us, and has to be won over to us by the pleading of the Son. This last difficulty I shall attempt to answer at a later stage, but to the other one about the inadequacy of our language I shall attempt to say now that we must be conscious today even more than ever that our words are inadequate, that they are at best the stumbling expression of a great mystery. But we believe that we *must* go on using them, as St. Augustine said in a similar context, we speak in order not to be silent. And we do maintain that they make a difference for us! Indeed, if they made no difference for our faith and our prayers, they would have no significance at all. So I shall try to present here with no elaborations of thought which cannot be "cashed" in the coinage of living worship, and hope, and faith.

With these two answers in our minds, let us go back to the argument of the letter to the Hebrews, and take from it what seems most relevant to our purpose. Here we must remember that all Christians submit themselves to the authority of the same text, even though their interpretations may still differ.

We saw how the writer to the Hebrews emphasised the superiority of the priesthood of Jesus to the Judaic priesthood of Old Testament days. In Christ, he tells us, all that God gave to his people under the forms of the old religion and priesthood, is both fulfilled and left behind. The Jewish priests sacrificed animals, not without God's ordinance, to make peace between a holy and righteous God and his sinful people. Yet these sacrifices had to be repeated again and again, and this itself was a mark of their provisional and inadequate character. But Christ offered his perfect sacrifice, once for all, and that sacrifice was accepted. There can be no doubt that this is the consistent teaching of Hebrews about Christ's sacrifice. It is teaching again and again repeated. The writer has no other teaching on this theme.

Here it will be necessary to quote only two chief typical passages. The first is this:[1]

"Every priest stands performing his service daily and offering time after time the same sacrifices, which can never remove sins. But Christ offered for all time one sacrifice for sins, and took his seat at the right hand of God, where he waits henceforth until his enemies are made his footstool. For by one offering he has perfected for all time those who are thus consecrated. Here we have also the testimony of the Holy Spirit: he first says: (Here the writer quotes the famous chapter from *Jeremiah* about the New Covenant,[2] which Jesus applied to himself.) 'This is the covenant which I will make with them after those days, says the Lord: I will set my laws in their hearts and write them in their understanding'; then he adds, 'and their sins and wicked deeds I will remember no more at all.' And where these have been forgiven, there is no longer any offering for sin."

The second passage is taken from *Hebrews* 9, vv. 24–28:

"Christ has entered . . . heaven itself to appear now before God on our behalf. Nor is he there to offer himself again and again, (on the day of Atonement) . . . with blood not his own. If that were so, he would have had to suffer many times since the world was made. But as it is, he has appeared once and for all at the climax of history to abolish sin by the sacrifice of himself. And as it is the lot of men to die once, and after death comes judgement, so Christ was offered once to bear the burden of men's sins . . ."

[1] *Hebrews* 10, vv. 11–18.
[2] *Jeremiah* 31, v. 31.

True, this offering is not only the death, but the incarnation, and the life, and all that leads up to the death, but it concluded, and was accepted by the Father when Christ passed into the unseen. This is his finished work. Nothing, absolutely nothing, can be admitted which would call in question the glorious certainty and finality of this deed. As Christopher Smart said in the last verse of his splendid Hymn to David:

> Glorious, more glorious is the crown
> Of Him that brought salvation down,
> By meekness called thy Son;
> Thou that stupendous truth believed,
> And now the matchless deed's achieved,
> Determined, dared, and done.

But the writer to the Hebrews continues further:

Though his sacrifice is complete, the *priesthood* of Christ is not finished; it continues in heaven, it continues under the form of intercession. Here Christ is like the Jewish priests whose task it was to intercede for their people. Yet Hebrews significantly makes Christ not stand as he presents his intercession to the Father, as would a suppliant uncertain of having his prayer granted. No! "When he had brought about purgation of sins, he took his seat at the right hand of the majesty on high."

At this point I quote again words of St. Augustine, "Who is so foolish as to believe that God has literally a right hand?" It is clear that a metaphor is being used. This place of honour, the seat at God's right hand, means that this Jesus whom we know, and who loves us, and whom in our feebleness we yet love and trust, as he came from the heart of God to us, has returned to the place of uttermost authority. And if it be right, as I think it is right, to think of him as interceding for us, then it is as one, who in obedience to his divine calling and his faithful obedience to his commission, can intercede with full assurance of the granting of his request. Surely then, the writer of the letter to the Hebrews is saying no more than St. Paul had so splendidly written already in the eighth chapter of *Romans*. "With all this in mind, what are we to say? If God is on our side, who is against us? He did not spare his own Son, but surrendered him for us all, and with this gift, how can he fail to lavish upon us all he has to give? It is God who pronounces acquittal, then who can condemn? It is Christ, Christ who died, and more than that, was raised from the dead, who is at God's right hand, and indeed pleads our cause. Then what can separate us from the love of Christ?"

But now we come to the difficulty which I mentioned before, and did not attempt to answer then, the difficulty of conceiving of Christ interceding for us. Does this not imply that the Father is hostile to us, and must be won over by the Son? Certainly any such idea, if necessarily implied in intercession, would make the whole conception impossible. It would deny the fact that is essential to the New Testament, that the Father's love is the basis and origin of the mission and priesthood of Jesus; it would introduce a fatal division between the Father and the Son.

But does intercession necessarily imply this division? When Christians intercede with God, is it not rather, to use MacLeod Campbell's fine expression rather "the drawing forth from the heart of the Father such blessings as he longs to give us", and it may be, as he has ordained things, *can* only give us in answer to prayer?

This is itself a great mystery, which is made much deeper still when we dare to apply the thought of intercession within the Holy Trinity itself, and there touch upon a theme whose significance we can perhaps more clearly feel than conceive. Yet both Paul and the writer to the Hebrews do not fail to touch upon it, Paul in the eighth chapter of *Romans* which I quoted. "It is Christ, Christ who died, and, more than that, was raised from the dead, who is at God's right hand, and indeed pleads our cause." And the writer to the Hebrews says, "The priesthood which Jesus holds is perpetual, because he remains for ever. That is why he is also able to save absolutely those who approach God through him, he is always living to plead on their behalf."[1]

About this continuing expression of Christ's priesthood in intercession the writer to the Hebrews speaks with a fitting reserve. He speaks of Christ's human experience as having qualified him for his eternal priesthood. It qualified him firstly because in his earthly life and death he made his perfect offering, and further through living and dying as a man he gained that human experience which equipped him for his heavenly intercession. He knows how to intercede for us, because he has gone every step of our journey himself. "Ours is not a high priest unable to sympathise with us in our weaknesses, but one who because of his likeness to us, has been tested every way, only without sin. Let us therefore boldly approach the

[1] Hebrews 7, vv. 24-5

69

throne of our gracious God, where we may receive mercy and in his grace find timely help."[1]

From this last quotation it would appear that Jesus' experiences as man, even to the final dereliction and death, qualify him for his continuing task of intercession. He knows how lonely man can be, for he was forsaken by all; he knows and can help us in bereavement and death, for he has been bereaved and he has died. And the human heart knows something of this too, for have we not felt in the moment when death was near, that a Saviour who had not gone through this would not be much help to us? He knows these things in a way that even the Almighty cannot know them. He has gone through them himself.

James Denney has said that from these words about Christ's temptations fitting him to supply us with help in time of need, we may conclude that Christ's intercession is not a continuous unvarying representation of man before God, but "relates itself sympathetically to the variously emergent necessities of individual life". So as Jesus said to Peter in the upper room, when Peter was about to face a particularly urgent temptation, "Simon, Simon, Satan hath desired to have you that he might sift you as wheat, but I have prayed for thee that thy faith fail not", in the same way he intercedes for us in the particular temptations and opportunities we meet today.

Having said this about the sacrifice that it is complete, once for all offered, and once for all accepted, we must go on to say that Christ's sacrifice is present with his intercession; eternal, not because eternally being offered, but

[1] *Hebrews* 4, vv. 15–16.

because once offered and accepted, it is the eternal basis and foundation of the intercession. It is to the Son who has completed his offering that the Father grants the prayers which he prays in filial confidence. He is the one commissioned to do so, and the Father in love answers his confident request of love.

If this be a true exposition of the teaching of the writer to the Hebrews, confirmed by the writings of St. Paul, then we may apply it to the Sacrament of the Lord's Supper. For the Christ who is present with us in the Sacrament is the Christ of whom we have been speaking; there is no other Christ.

His sacrifice is present with him in the sense that he is the Christ who in his life and death offered his sacrifice. Therefore the words in the Consecration Prayer of our Communion Service where we speak of – "Pleading his eternal sacrifice" – cannot mean that we plead with the Father to accept the Son's sacrifice. They must express our admission that without this gift we would not have this access to the Father, and they must come from a background, as it were, of humble gratitude that we do in fact have this gift, which we never could have seized for ourselves.

Christ's sacrifice has been accepted. Therefore we cannot offer it again; it is God's gift to us, which we in our turn must accept. How absurd, even insulting, it would be to offer back to a human friend a precious gift which he had given to us at the greatest cost to himself! The only thing to do is to receive such a gift with humble gratitude. To think of our offering Christ's sacrifice, or sharing in offering it, is like trying to push open a door which already stands wide open to us, and which we could never have unlocked for ourselves.

This is what Calvin indicates when he says, "As widely as giving differs from receiving, does sacrifice differ from the sacrament."[1] And this is precisely what Luther meant when he said that the sacrifice of the Mass, as he saw it, turned upside down the nature of a Sacrament.

Yet there are two things which the Church can do, and which we can do in the Sacrament, and with the mention of these I shall bring this chapter to a close.

There is a sense in which we in the Church do offer a sacrifice in the Sacrament, and that is the first thing. When I say this I withdraw nothing of what has already been said. What we offer is our praise, and ourselves. Calvin himself agrees fully on this point, and the Westminster Confession says that in the Sacrament a spiritual oblation or offering – of all possible praise is made unto God for the one offering of Christ by himself upon the cross. This we could never have done unless he had given himself for us, nor can we present a perfect sacrifice as it is. "Not as we ought, but as we are able, do we bless thee for his holy incarnation" – says the prayer of consecration in our *Book of Common Order*, representing a tradition that goes back to the Clementine Liturgy of the fourth century A.D.[2]

And this offering of gratitude cannot be sincere unless it includes an offering of our wills and ourselves to God.

[1] *John Calvin Institutes*, IV, 18. 7.
[2] *Apostolic Constitutions*, Bk. VIII, ch. 12; Clark, *Ante Nicene Christian Library*, Vol. XVII, Edinburgh.

Were the whole realm of Nature mine,
That were an offering far too small;
Love so amazing, so divine,
Demands my soul, my life, my all.[1]

And while we present our offering, not his, which has
been already offered and accepted, there is no doubt
that he presents our praise, and with it, our self-dedication
to the Father, interceding for us as he does so, and willing
that our feeble intercessions should ascend to the Father
with his own in the Spirit.

And this is the second thing that I have to say, with
which I shall conclude this chapter. We cannot offer
Christ's sacrifice to God, for it is God's gift to us. But we
can and must *intercede* with the Father on the basis and
strength of it. To do this is nothing more than to appropriate the gift, to enter upon our sonship, to enter upon
and take possession of that filial relation with the Father
which God gives us through his Son, and which the Son
invites us to share. Christ makes, as it were, a place beside
himself for us, asking that we share it with him, as with
him we look to the Father in obedience and trust and
hope.

This freedom of sonship and daughterhood is indeed
open to us at all times, but never more so than in the
Holy Communion when we intercede with the Father
through the Son, aided by the Spirit of God himself.
Our prayers are then made for our friends; and then they
move out beyond our circle to all who are in need in
God's vast kingdom, asking in the words of the

[1] *Church Hymnary*, Hymn 106.

73

Communion Consecration Prayer "that thou wilt fulfil in us and all men the purpose of thy redeeming love."[1] Here every barrier falls away, and we stretch out our hands towards the consummation of the ages.

[1] *Book of Common Order*, p. 120.

CHAPTER V

The Lord's Supper as a Sign of Hope

"In that night they were saved, and in that night they shall be saved." This striking old Jewish saying, taken almost from Jesus' own time, points back to the Passover night in Egypt, when the Lord led out his people from captivity "with a high hand and an outstretched arm". And it points forward to the coming of the Messiah to deliver his people. He would come on Passover night – might it not be this very Passover night?

And St. Jerome, writing in the fourth century, says, "The tradition of the Jews is that Christ will come in the middle of the night, just as he did in the time of Egypt, at the Passover season." It has also been pointed out that during the time of the Roman domination, the rebellions against the occupying Power were apt to occur at Passover time. These rebellions were often led by false Messiahs, and perhaps the sedition in which Barabbas was taken prisoner was just such a Messianic revolt.[1]

This last suggestion is conjecture, but there is no doubt as to the main point; Passover time was a time when hopes of the coming Messiah ran high. Thus, when Jesus and his disciples sat down at the Passover meal in the upper room, we can be sure of one thing; mysterious hopes for the

[1] *Mark* 15, v. 7. cf. Jeremias, *The Eucharistic Words of Jesus*, 3rd edn., pp. 205–7.

future, coming out of ancient Jewish tradition, were in the hearts of the disciples, as well as the memory of God's past deliverance of their people.

But it is clear that Jesus' own actions and his teaching had in the preceding months given a special encouragement to these Messianic hopes connected with the Passover. The Gospels tell us a good deal about the rivalries among the disciples in the weeks before Christ's death, and even on the night of his betrayal. What was the cause of these rivalries? Each of the disciples wanted to be a leader in the new Kingdom of God which was dawning. They were arguing amongst themselves as to who should have the right to sit on Jesus' right hand and his left in the positions of honour at the Messianic feast.

There can, indeed, be little doubt that the hope of the coming Kingdom of God and the victory of his cause was central both to the thought of Jesus and his disciples, and to that of the primitive church. And at no place and at no time did this light burn more intensely than in the upper room on the night of the Last Supper. Nor is it possible to eradicate this hope from the Sacrament of the Last Supper which has been handed down to us through the centuries. It is this aspect of the Supper which is our theme in the present chapter.

But it is just at this point that a whole nest of difficulties is uncovered; difficulties which we ourselves have felt and which are shared by a host of honest and intelligent people. Let us imagine one of them putting them to us. "You talk quite happily about these hopes of a triumphant close to history, this outlook upon a splendid future. You are even giving this theme the final place, the place of honour in your book. Yet you must confess that these hopes, which Jesus seems to have shared, were unfulfilled. The glorious reign of God did not come. And this failure in fulfilment is bad enough, but there is worse to come. The fact is, that today we simply cannot think any longer in images of the kind that Jesus and the New Testament writers use."

Now there are Christian thinkers who are so impressed by these difficulties that they feel themselves forced to agree with this opinion. They point out that these hopes of a coming Day of the Lord arose in Jewish hearts under long stress of disappointment and suffering under foreign domination, with

> Right for ever on the scaffold,
> Wrong for ever on the throne.

They concede that the expectation of a day when the Lord would vindicate his own people gave comfort in their day to sorely tried men and women. But they aver that they give no help to *our* faith, indeed they are rather a hindrance.

However these outworn ideas may be expressed, they say, it makes no difference. Whether we speak of a second coming of Christ, or of the defeat of all the powers of evil, or of every knee bowing to Christ, and every tongue confessing that he is Lord, or whether we speak of the whole creation standing on tiptoe to see the revelation of the sons of God, it is all one. We may use the grotesque imagery of St. Paul in *Thessalonians* about trumpets sounding, and God descending with a shout, or we may employ less offensive language, it all makes no odds. It all belongs to that queer brand of thinking which flourished before and after the time of Christ, and which scholars describe as Jewish Apocalyptic, and which paints in lurid colours the end of all things. No matter what we call it, we can't be doing with it any more, so we must just get along without the idea of a grand *finale*, and the ringing down of the curtain on the great drama, in which justice will be finally vindicated, and evil will surrender unconditionally.

These men are themselves Christians, and they believe that while we must jettison all this imagery, there does remain the fact that Christ has placed before us the offer of God's forgiveness, and the challenge of a new life in faith, and that as we accept it we step out into the future and a freedom from the bad entail of our past. But all this is a possibility *now*, and there remains nothing more for the future to give except this – that we can and must every day and every hour accept this gift anew. Every thing else of which we have spoken, every picture of a triumph in or beyond history must be discarded as a myth that men of the twentieth century should not be asked to believe, for with all the will in the world, they simply cannot.[1]

But there are others who do not accept these arguments, and I am with them. Emil Brunner is one of them, and I might summarise what he says on this matter, as follows, "This whole idea of a triumphant end is no mere phantasy called forth from the imagination of the Jewish race under the pressure of foreign domination. It is something that belongs to the very essence both of the Jewish faith,

[1] This is, I hope, a fair description of the views on this point of Rudolf Bultmann and his school.

and still more of the Christian faith. Our God, the living God of Christian faith, differs from the conceptions of God current in the religions, by this one thing above all else, that he is the God with a goal, the goal of the Kingdom, or rule, of God. That is, he is the God who not only enters into history but directs history towards his goal."[1]

Brunner continues: "When we are drawn to faith in God, we are drawn into this movement of his towards his goal. This goal is pictured in various ways, as the future coming of Christ, the consummation of all things, the arrival at the end of the journey. Faith in Jesus without the hope of this consummation is a cheque that can never be cashed, a promise that is not made in earnest, a flight of stairs that leads nowhere, but ends in the void. As an expectant mother carries within her the child that is to be born, so faith carries *this* future within it. A faith which is not some day to be transcended in sight is not faith at all, but illusion." Thus far Dr. Brunner.

Now it is true that the future which we must await with such certainty, is one to which none of our pictures can do justice. It is in this respect different from all other futures. Of course, there are differing pictures given of it in the New Testament, and we need not trouble overmuch if they cannot be neatly dovetailed together to form one coherent whole. For we know that none of them can be exact or adequate, nor do they claim to be so; they are confessedly attempts to portray the inconceivable, arrows shot out towards the transcendent reality. One

[1] Brunner, *Dogmatics, III, English Translation*, pp. 339–46. London, 1962.

of the most famous of them is the picture of a return of
exiles to their home country. This is a picture taken
from the historical memory of the Jewish people whom
God had brought back in a marvellous way from exile in
Babylon. "Many shall come in from the east and west,
and shall sit down with Abraham, and Isaac, and Jacob,
in the kingdom of heaven."[1]

Another, still more famous, and still more apposite
in our present context, is the picture of a great feast, which
indeed is probably hinted at in the sentence just quoted.
Just as our pictures of this final triumph of grace and
judgement, use language which we know cannot be
precise or exact, so it is also true that the figures which the
New Testament uses to describe it are often taken from
the apocalyptic literature of which I have spoken. But
this does not mean, as some think, that the hope itself is
discredited because the inadequacy of the images is now
more clearly realised than ever before. The hope remains
bound to the Christian faith as so essential to it, that if this
hope be destroyed, the faith is not merely weakened, its
very back is broken.

Therefore we must not dismiss as mere Jewish "old
clothes" the Messianic hopes which pervade the account
of the Last Supper. It is no exaggeration to say that it
looks forward to the consummation of all things, and the
event which it calls the Lord's return, like a face turned
eagerly to the sunrise.

Since the Passover feast through the centuries had been
full of these hopes, and the ministry of Jesus had accentu-
ated them among his disciples, we would expect the

[1] *Matthew* 8, v. 11.

accounts of the Last Supper to be suffused with the same intense glow of hope, a hope all the more radiant by reason of its contrasts with the utter darkness of the impending death of Jesus, and the apprehensions of the disciples. And this is in fact what we find. As it has been said: "At the nadir of defeat and solitude, Jesus founds a rite, and sends it down through all history, a rite which will be a continual prophecy of victory."[1]

It is in Luke's account that this note sounds out most clearly, but it is also present in *Mark* and *Matthew*, and, also, indirectly, in Paul's account in *1 Corinthians* 11, appearing there as a comment of the apostle himself. He writes there, "For every time you eat this bread, and drink this cup, you proclaim the death of the Lord, until he comes."

We have now come to the point in our argument when a closer examination of the accounts of the Last Supper must be made, this time with a view to bringing into prominence this forward look into a transcendent future, which is common to them all. The first account to consider is that of St. Luke, who writes thus – "When the time came he took 'his place at table, and the apostles with him, and he said to them, 'How I have longed to eat this Passover with you before my death! For I tell you, never again shall I eat it until the time when it finds its fulfilment in the Kingdom of God.'"[2]

From these words we can get a deep insight into the mind of Jesus. We know that already he was convinced

[1] David Cairns, *An Autobiography*, London, S.C.M. Press 1950, p. 201.
[2] *Luke* 22, vv. 14–16.

that his Covenant was the fulfilment of the Old Testament Covenant. Here he goes further, and says that the Messianic feast will fulfil all that was promised in the Old Testament Passover, and also all that is promised in the New Covenant which he is now instituting.

Luke continues with the following words, "Then he took a cup, and after giving thanks, he said, 'Take this, and share it among yourselves, for I tell you, from this moment I shall drink of the fruit of the vine no more until the time when the kingdom of God comes.'"[1]

At this point no English version can do justice to the vehemence of the twice repeated negative of the Greek, and it has been pointed out that what we have here is, in effect, a solemn vow made by Jesus. Such solemn vows were not infrequent among the Jews, both in Old Testament and New Testament times. On one occasion King Saul made his warriors swear that none of them would eat before the evening, when complete victory in battle had been won, and his own son Jonathan innocently came under the curse invoked by his father on anyone who broke his fast before that hour.[2]

The most striking New Testament instances of such oaths, apart from the one we are now considering, both concern the apostle Paul. One of them was apparently a vow made by him that he would not cut his hair until he left Corinth – thus apparently making clear to the Church at Corinth that, though they had pressed him to stay, his intention to depart was irrevocable.[3]

[1] *Luke* 22, vv. 17–18.
[2] *1 Samuel* 14, vv. 24–46.
[3] *Acts* 18, v. 18.

The other case was that of the "more than forty" men in Jerusalem, who took an oath that they would neither eat nor drink until they had killed Paul.[1]

Jeremias asks if we can conjecture why Jesus should have taken this vow of abstinence, and concludes that he wished to make it quite clear to his disciples that he had taken an irrevocable decision, to open up the way for the Kingdom of God by his death for others, "He burns his bridges, forswears feasting and wine, and prepares himself with resolute will to drink the bitter cup which the father offers him. A man who will never eat or drink again has said goodbye to this world. Now his life-work is almost finished, now he belongs wholly to the coming kingdom of God." And Jeremias goes on to ask whether he refused to drink the drugged wine offered to him on the cross, because this would have been to break his vow.[2]

And, further, pursuing the same line of thought, we may ask whether Jesus may not, by this vow, have desired to give the disciples the assurance that the time of his absence from them would not mean that he had forgotten them, or was inactive, but that in the unseen world the whole urgency of his will, and perhaps we may add, of his intercessions, would be set to hasten the coming of God's triumph.

In this passage Mark gives a slightly different version

[1] *Acts* 23, v. 21.

[2] *Mark*, 15 v. 23. *The Eucharistic Words of Jesus*, E.T., 1st edition, p. 171. In the 3rd edition of his book *The Eucharistic Words of Jesus*, E.T. 1966, p. 216, Jeremias suggests a new interpretation of the significance of this vow, but does not deny the possibility of his former interpretation.

from Luke, "I tell you this; never again shall I drink from the fruit of the vine until the day when I drink it new (Matthew adds 'with you') in the Kingdom of God."[1] The word for "new" in the Greek (kainos) is a special word, which we may take it to indicate that it will be a redeemed and transfigured world in which the feast is celebrated.

At this point Luke goes on to tell how even now a dispute about priority arose among the disciples, and how Jesus told them that the greatest among them was to bear himself as the servant of all – as he himself was doing, concluding with the words "and now I vest in you the kingship which my Father vested in me; you shall eat and drink at my table in my kingdom, and sit on thrones as judges of the twelve tribes of Israel".[2] From all of this it is surely clear beyond question that the Sacrament as Christ instituted it emphasised the great hope of the future just as intensely as it does the memory of the past and the communion in the present.

We now come to the words of St. Paul in *1 Corinthians* 11, words first of Jesus himself, followed by words of interpretation by St. Paul. "Do this in remembrance (or, as a memorial) of me. For every time you eat this bread, and drink this cup, you proclaim the death of the Lord, until He comes."

Here, as in connection with nearly every detail of the New Testament dealing with the Sacrament, there is hardly a word which has not been interpreted diversely, hardly a word about which there has not been passionate

[1] *Mark* 14, v. 25.
[2] *Luke* 22, v. 29.

contention. On the whole I have tried to avoid raising such contentious issues which lend themselves little to devotion. But here an exception may be made. There are two main interpretations of these words. There are those who say that this proclamation and memorial cannot be anything but a proclaiming to men, and a memorial before them. And there are those who claim that the words "this do in remembrance of me", or "as a memorial of me" signify not merely a memorial before men, but one before God. Such is the interpretation of Jeremias and of Max Thurian, though it is contested by scholars of equal eminence. Jeremias suggests that Jesus enjoins this memorial upon his followers, in order that God may remember him, that is, may bring about the consummation of all things for which he is about to suffer his death. And Jeremias backs his suggestion with a wealth of evidence from the Old Testament to prove that this was the sense of "a memorial" in many instances mentioned there.

There are those who fear that such teaching will inevitably lead us back to a false view of the Lord's Supper from which the Reformation set us free. We must recall that at the time of the Reformation the Roman Church claimed that it had the power to offer Christ to his Father in the sacrifice of the Mass for the sins of the living and the dead in such a way that the stay of souls in purgatory could be shortened by such Masses said on their behalf. Surely any claim to take issues out of the hand of God would be blasphemous, and would be made worse, if possible, where those who celebrated such Masses did it for money.

Yet no Christian can deny that believers are called on by God to intercede, or that, though God retains his own sovereignty, he has promised to answer intercession. And since the Sacrament is above all other times the occasion when we remember God's gift to us in Christ, and thank him for it, then surely it should also be the supreme occasion when, on the strength of that great gift, we intercede for others. And especially it should be the time when we pray for the culmination of all God's gifts in the victory of Christ's kingdom.

Is there anything here but the fullest evangelical truth? Is what I have indicated more than the turning into prayer of Paul's great words, "If God is on our side, who is against us? He did not spare his own Son, but surrendered him for us all, and with this gift, how can he fail to lavish upon us all he has to give?"[1]

Again, is this teaching not merely an expansion of the beginning of the Lord's Prayer, "Our Father, which art in heaven . . . Thy kingdom come"? For the first two words, "Our Father" summarise the whole gift that God has made to us in Christ. It is he who has revealed to us the Fatherhood of God; it is he who has opened up to us the new humanity with its liberty of access to God in prayer, both prayer for others and ourselves. Thanking God for him and the new humanity which he has given to us – or restored to us – we enter into that humanity and pray "Thy Kingdom come."

Objections have been made to the idea that the sacrament is a memorial before the Father, and they have been based on two grounds.

[1] *Romans* 8, vv. 31–32.

86

First, it has been averred that the idea of such a memorial before the Father is unworthy of the New Testament conception of God. It is said that it suggests that the Father is hostile to us, and needs to be appeased, by having the Son's merits pled to him.

Secondly, opponents of the view that this is a memorial before the Father, quote with approval indignant words used by John Knox to the Romanists of his own day in a somewhat similar context. "Is there any oblivion or forgetfulness fallen on God the Father? Hath he forgotten the death and passion of Jesus Christ so that he need to be brought in memory thereof by any mortal man?"[1]

Both these objections, if they could be sustained, would indeed be fatal. In point of fact, neither of them is valid. Not, at least, if the memorial is regarded in the sense here taken, as an act of intercession. In the first place, as I indicated in the fourth chapter, Christian intercession is never to be regarded as an attempt to win over an unwilling or angry God. It is the drawing forth from the Father, by his own desire, of the blessings which he has bidden us to ask of him, and which he longs to give us, and which, in some cases, maybe, he can only give to those who ask of him. Such intercession is no rival to the finished work of Christ in reconciling God and man. On the contrary, it is based and founded on the gift that God has given to us in him. It is, in fact, the use of the free access Christ has achieved for us to the Father, as sharers in his own humanity.

---

[1] *John Knox* by Lord Eustace Percy, London (1937), cited by W. M. F. Scott, *Theology* LVI, No. 400, October 1953, p. 387.

Secondly, the notion that our view implies that God has forgotten Christ is also unrealistic. It may be that in very early days Old Testament men may have believed that God actually forgot them, and had to be reminded by prayer and sacrifice. But surely such a crude view was very early transcended. When the Bible says that God remembered a man, or a nation, it surely does not mean that until that moment God had for a time forgotten them. How would this be consistent with the Bible's teaching that God knows everything? When the Bible writers used the words "God remembered" in this context, they mean that God acts to vindicate that person or people whom he "remembers", and vindicates himself by saving and delivering them.

So that if Jesus did say "Pray that God will remember me", he did not imply that the Father would forget him if this was not done. His meaning was that the Christian Church, in celebrating the Sacrament should intercede with the Father for the consummation of the greatest blessing of all, the perfect coming of the Kingdom, which he had already made sure through the finished work of Christ. The measure of what the Father has already done is to be the measure of our confidence, when we pray that he will complete his work with mankind and with the world.

When this will happen or how it will happen we cannot tell. Not only are these things, as Jesus said to his disciples, concerns which "the Father hath put in his own power",[1] but also the fulfilment of his purpose is bound to be one that will transcend the conditions of time and

[1] *Acts* 1, v. 7.

space as we understand them. Yet to this inconceivable and glorious fulfilment we must look forward, for it is the culmination of what has been given to us already, and the assurance that we have of its coming is bound up with the assurance of our faith in Christ himself.

Epilogue

We have now reached the end of our study. I hope that it may help to open the doors of experience for some of my readers as the reading and meditation underlying it have certainly done for myself. Reflection on the Christian Sacrament turns out in the end to be nothing less than reflection on the whole mystery of the Christian faith. And if we use here the term "mystery", we are using it in the pregnant sense given to it by the New Testament writers. St. Paul uses it to describe the loving plan of God, hidden from the beginning, but now made known to man, and stretching forward into a future which includes not only mankind, but the whole created world. Christians believe that this plan of God underlies the existence of the whole human race, and that it unfolds through the ages, overruling human error and sin. It is this conviction which gives the Christian faith its power to restore hope and assurance in the confused and fear-ridden world of today. Through the Sacrament we are not only given a vantage point of understanding about the plan, but are also able to take our place in it as the beneficiaries, sharing as heirs in a magnificent inheritance, and entering together into the privileges of membership in God's family.

If now, looking back, we trace the steps by which we have come hither, we shall see ourselves united with the

people of Israel who were brought into covenant with
God long ago – a covenant which began to take visible
shape in the early history of the Hebrew people. In this
remembered past there are things which bear clearly the
marks of the childhood of our race, just as we, today,
looking into our early childhood, can recognise that
many of our memories bear on them the traces of infancy.
They are not, and in the nature of the case, could not be,
memories such as could have originated in the experience
of a grown man. Yet, in the case of the individual, this
fact does not discredit the whole story of his remembered
past, and mark it as mythical. For, however much the
element of the childish and the primitive may pervade
our own memories of childhood, there remains for us as
something fundamental in them, the knowledge of our
relationship with our parents. If we were fortunate in our
parents, this relationship was one of love and care given
by them, and accepted or assumed by us as natural. On
this relationship, expressed in remembered actions, our
whole life was built up, and the relationship was not called
in question.

So also is it with the story of the Hebrew people. Behind
all its memories of its origin – in which there is undoubt-
edly a mixture of primitive and mythical elements – there
remains the enduring certainty of the covenant with God,
who took and retained the initiative, whose truth con-
sisted in the fact that he was always present in grace
and judgement, and would never betray his people's
trust.

In the Passover Sacrament, these men of the Old
Testament were called on to thank God for what he had

done for them in the Passover deliverance, in order that they might venture forth into the future, trusting themselves to the love of the God who had so befriended them, and was still summoning them out into the unknown.

When Jesus instituted the Sacrament, he was bringing the drama into its second act: calling his followers to remember the great deeds of God achieved, and shortly to be achieved, by himself. He was admitting them – and potentially with them, mankind as a whole, into a new sonship of God, and a sharing of his own humanity. All this was the theme of our first chapter.

In the second chapter we reflected on the nature of the presence of Christ in the Sacrament, and the gift which he offers, while in the third we considered a further aspect of that gift, the fellowship which is there opened up for us with Christ, with each other, and with all Christian people, and with those who are in heaven.

The fourth chapter dealt with a theme on which there is more difference among Christian people – the place of sacrifice and intercession in the Lord's Supper. Here we recognised the difficulty of the whole idea of sacrifice for men and women of the twentieth century, but came to the conclusion that it was one idea, which, among others, was necessary for a full understanding of what Jesus has done for us. Here, holding fast to the belief that he has completed his work of sacrifice on our behalf, and that we cannot offer his sacrifice to the Father, much less add to it, we claimed that our duty is to receive that gift gratefully from him, and use it. Yet though at this point we felt that the teaching of the High Churchmen could not be accepted, there seemed to be a poverty in the alternative presented by certain members of the Evangelical Party, and we concluded that we could do justice to a genuine concern of the High Churchmen by claiming that we can share in the priestly work of Christ in intercession for the coming of God's kingdom. This is a chief function of the Sacrament.

So, having spanned human history in remembrance of the past, communion in the present, and prayer for the future, we turned our eyes to the Sacrament as a sign of Christian hope, suggesting that though the images and symbols which we are forced to use in expressing this hope are confessedly inadequate, yet the hope itself cannot be surrendered. For in what is already given to us in the presence and the gift, there lies the assurance that some day we shall have the same gift and presence, but at last no longer in a form in which they are concealed, and only apprehended by faith, but possessed and seen face to face.

So the story ends with a look into the future. Here, as in the case of the Passover beginnings, the detail is obscure, but for a different reason. There the obscurity came from the immaturity of the people bound in covenant to God in the dawn of history. The obscurity with regard to the transcendent future arises from our continuing immaturity *now*. This is a limitation necessary to our human condition, but one that we expect will some day be overcome in the day of open vision. Then we may well realise, looking backward, just in what manner all the images we had used on earth to picture the transcendent future were in their different ways inadequate.

But we shall probably agree, in that day when we can compare these images with the directly experienced reality, that such were the only terms in which, under the conditions of earthly life, we could in some measure apprehend it.

The present climate of thought in the world seems to have two characteristics different from the climate of earlier days. It is certain that neither of them was present at the time of Robert Bruce, the minister of St. Giles Cathedral who was mentioned in the Introduction, who conversed and contended with his royal master, King James the Sixth and First. One of these characteristics may be set down as helpful for our understanding of the Sacrament, and the other as distinctly hostile to it.

It is a little difficult to describe these two factors clearly. But the helpful one may be described as the demand that all our language, if it is to be regarded as meaningful, must at least make some difference to our outlook on life, our actions, our understanding of ourselves, and of our environment. This requirement is surely a salutary curb on idle speculation and refinement by means of subtle distinctions. This kind of speculation has often led thought, and especially thought about divine things, to get right out of touch with realities. Such idle and fanciful thought-spinning is itself a sign of irreverence in the presence of the mysteries of the world. In writing this little book I have been often forced to ask myself – what difference does this or that distinction of the theologians make to the communion of Christian people with God?

Such a hostility to arid speculations as is current in the world today can do little but good to theological and devotional thought.

The other factor, which does not help us, but rather hinders us, curiously springs from the same mental climate, from a habit of thinking which limits the meaningful to that which can be verified. For, proceeding on too narrow a conception of verification, there are many thinkers today who have forgotten that our existence and this world through which we are travellers is full of mystery.

In writing these chapters I have tried to indicate that we are here dealing with profound mysteries which we can only describe and explain inadequately, and which we have no right to dismiss as mumbo-jumbo where we cannot fully comprehend them. At the same time I have tried to seek an entrance to the meaning of these mysteries which will at least enable the reader to begin to understand them, so that he will not feel that anything has here been written which provokes him to a justified revolt of reason against unreason. There are interpretations of such matters as eating the flesh and drinking the blood of Christ which seem at least to me to border upon the blasphemous.

In conclusion we must take courage from the fact that full comprehension of these mysteries is luckily not required for those who are still travelling on their way through life. And it is for them that the Sacrament is intended. We must comfort ourselves with the reflection that the men to whom Jesus with his own hands gave the Sacrament of his body and blood, understood on that night very little of the significance of his gift, but that in all their uncertainty and sinfulness they at least knew that their hearts were with him, and that they loved him. If a man knows this, then he is ready to come to communion.